Penny Boss

'Who lost these?' I ask, holding up the pair of knickers. There is an uncanny silence from the infant class, full of disapproving undercurrents.

'Who lost these?' I repeat.

The finder stands at my elbow, hoping there will be no claimant just yet, and then he will be able to tour the whole school seeking one, and have a pleasant recreation.

The word they all consider shocking must be used to produce some reaction, so I shout, 'Who lost these *knickers*?'

The combined whisper that comes from the back of the class is horrified.

'The Minister – !'

I swing round, still holding up the seductive pants – almost under the noses of the Headmaster and a man wearing a clerical collar. . . .

By the same author in Arrow

Penny Buff

Janetta Bowie

Penny Boss

A Clydeside school in the 'fifties

ARROW BOOKS

Arrow Books Limited
3 Fitzroy Square, London WIP 6JD

An imprint of the Hutchinson Publishing Group

London Melbourne Sydney Auckland
Wellington Johannesburg and agencies
throughout the world

First published by Constable and Company Limited 1976
Arrow edition 1979
© Janetta Bowie 1976

Made and printed in Great Britain by The Anchor Press Ltd
Tiptree, Essex

ISBN 0 09 918640 3

April
1947

'Who lost these?' I ask, holding up the pair of knickers. There is an uncanny silence from the infant class, full of disapproving undercurrents.

'Who lost these?' I repeat.

The finder stands at my elbow, hoping there will be no claimant just yet, and then he will be able to tour the whole school seeking one, and have a pleasant recreation.

The word they all consider shocking must be used to produce some reaction, so I shout, 'Who lost these *knickers*?'

The combined whisper that comes from the back of the class is horrified.

'The Minister – !'

I swing round, still holding up the seductive pants – almost under the noses of the Headmaster and a man wearing a clerical collar.

'Here – ' I thrust the knickers into the hands of the finder and hiss, 'try Miss McMenamie.'

The face above the clerical collar grins broadly.

'I'm afraid we stole in upon you unawares,' says the Head. 'Let me introduce the Rev Andrew McGowan.'

'Sorry to come upon you,' the Rev Andrew says, 'in an embarrassing moment.'

We shake hands, and I find he is the firm-grasping, boys'-club kind of clergyman.

'Mr McGowan is from the Education Committee,' the Head says. 'He'll be visiting the school from time to time – just to see how we're all getting on, you know. I've been telling Mr McGowan that you've been trying out new methods.'

To Mr McGowan he says, 'It's all a matter of different attitudes nowadays, of course.'

They both move towards Miss McMenamie's room. Her door is set in the glass partition between our two classes. The Rev McGowan, who I think must be about my own age, neither too old nor too young, shakes hands with me again as the Head opens Miss McMenamie's door. I glance quickly through to see if she is holding up the knickers, but the Head obscures my view.

'New attitudes, right enough,' says the Minister. 'Not afraid of the teacher any more. In my day,' he adds, edging through the door, 'the teachers used to scare the pants off us – '

The door closes upon them before I have time to register a facial reaction.

In the staffroom at the interval I deplore my ill-luck. 'To think,' I say, 'if I happen to be on that short list for the Infants Mistress-ship of Cresswell School, it's that Minister I'll see on the Education Committee! Whoever sent Tommy MacNab round the school with those pants?'

But nobody in the staffroom at the moment admits to it.

'You needn't worry about meeting your Minister again,' says Bella McSkimming, 'for you're not likely to be on any short list – so dinna fash yersel', hen.'

'You never know,' I say, forever hopeful, even in the teeth of embarrassing clergymen.

6

'You need to be at least sixty years of age before they'll even look at you for a post,' says Miss Grott.

'Are they all men on the Promotion Committee?'

'Mostly.'

'Then don't you think that they're more likely to look at a young – sorry, younger – woman than at an old one?'

'They're only after your teaching experience, not your virtue,' says Bet Dodd.

'Education Committees are impervious to female wiles,' says Bella.

'Maybe because the females in their experience are so dull,' I say determinedly.

'Far too many clergymen on Education Committees,' goes on Miss Grott, without variation on her favourite theme. 'And if you can find one woman among them on the day of the interview, you'll be lucky.'

'You'll be unlucky,' says Bella. 'Women vote against women. You're quite right to appeal to the men.'

'The Rev Andrew McGowan didn't strike me as being – impervious,' I contend.

'Is he married?' asks Bet, her big blue eyes rolling as if stricken.

But nobody is able to tell her that.

On the way to our classrooms Bet asks if I have written to any member of the Committee to advance what she calls my claim.

'I shouldn't dare!'

'Then do it,' she says. 'My brother believes in canvassing.'

'Really? But is it allowed?'

'Of course it is – in practice, anyway. It's always done. Didn't you read the Memorandum that came round intimating the post?'

'I just read the bit that said I should get £65 a year more salary as Infants Mistress of Cresswell.'

'Then you should have read the rest of it.'

I go to my desk and take out the Memorandum: 'Candidates may write to members of Committee, but may not call upon them, unless by invitation.'

'See! There it is!' says Bet.

'What will I say?'

'Tell them how well qualified you are. Send them testimonials.'

'I haven't got any. All I ever had are eighteen years out of date – old schoolgirl things.'

'Then dig out somebody who knew you of yore and get him to write up a good fiction yarn, all up-to-date, saying how distinguished you've become.'

'I couldn't really do that. I can't think of anybody.'

'Get your last Headmaster to do you a write-up.'

'He's dead. And I'm scared to even tell this one.'

'Well – what about old Pa McQuistan who tried so hard to teach you maths in the High School?'

'The fact that he had to try so hard wouldn't endear me to him.'

'Then what about Biddy Benson? She thought you were at least good at English. She's still in the High.'

'She was terribly absent-minded. She must have forgotten all about me by this time.'

'Then go and see her tonight and remind her.'

'How many people must I write to?'

'Oh – dozens! My brother Angus sent off a whole batch of letters the time he was promoted to First Assistant at Bonnyriggs.'

'Will anybody really invite me to visit him?'

'Of course. And if you know anybody who'll put in a word for you to the rest of the members, all the better. Didn't Peg's mother have a sweetheart from the long ago who was on the Committee at the time Peg came out of College? Remember, when we came out and jobs were scarce.'

'My mother didn't.'

'Then go and ask Peg's.'

'It's you who should be applying for this job, not me. Seems like a lot of intrigue to me.'

'Then learn to be intriguing. It's one way of getting out of Garlock St. Most of us haven't your excuse.'

'You have the Infants Mistress Certificate, too.'

'True. But that's only one of a number I have. I'll use some of the others first.'

8

I go home and begin my campaign. I first visit Miss Bedelia Benson – Biddy, as we called her. She remembers me at once. She is quite sure I shall make the great Infants Mistress of the future. She meticulously writes down all the information I can supply about my career since leaving her class in the High School. Every certificate I have ever gained at school or University is noted down, be it first, second or third class.

'We must tell all,' she says. 'You say you got a University prize too. Good. Good. Very difficult to get University prizes.'

'It had nothing to do with my teaching. Don't you think we'd better not – '

'Nonsense! Sounds impressive. I must have something substantial to work on. I'll send it on soon.'

May, 1947

I am immensely bucked up, to appointment pitch, in fact, when I get Biddy's testimonial this morning. It is more than flattering. It is incandescent. I show it to Bet.

'You're as good as appointed.'

'Nonsense! All these things happened to me in prehistoric times. I don't recognize myself. I couldn't flog that around.'

'Don't be an ass. Make a lot of copies. I got my brother Stephen to give me the list of members' names and addresses. Men are ruthless campaigners. You must be ruthless.'

'But there are thirty-six names on that list! I don't know a single one – except Andrew McGowan, and I couldn't possibly write to him.'

'Why not?'

'Because – well – because of – '

'Oh, you mean the – '

'Yes.'

'Of course! You nearly gave the lost garment to him. Oh, he'll have forgotten all about that.'

'I couldn't write out the testimonial thirty-six times. And I haven't a typewriter.'

'Then why don't you select any six, and do these tonight? Let

9

me see. Yes, Stephen has put an asterisk at those who are good at giving interviews.'

I look at the list of names.

'There are two asterisks at that one. The Rev Horace Pickering. Who is he?'

'He's an Episcopalian – a rector – or a canon – or an archdeacon – or something. He always gives an interview.'

'Really?'

'But he lives away up on Broadlaw Moor. It's an hour in the train, then half an hour's walk, I think.'

'If I ever get this job, I'll have deserved it. What a lot of Reverends there are!'

'You'd better brush up your Bible Knowledge then.'

'Do they really ask about that?'

'They might. Do you teach in the Sunday School?'

'I couldn't say "yes" to that. Look here, I think I'll withdraw my application.'

'Don't be a fool. If you pull it off, you'll be appointed to one of the biggest Infant Departments in the district. What's more, you'll be able to boss five other teachers. Think of that now!'

'I'd maybe better wait till a smaller school is advertised.'

'Oh, go on! Be a pioneer!'

Just as we are talking outside our classrooms, the Head appears at the top of the stairs and looks down at us significantly. We disappear immediately into our rooms. I have not dared to tell him that I have applied for promotion – not yet. That is one of the few things that Staff can do behind the Head's back.

I slave all night composing a sort of contradictory letter to members of the Committee, including the Rev Horace Pickering. Contradictory, because it strives to be modest and at the same time boasts shamefully about my qualifications. I read each of the six copies through before putting them into envelopes. Reading about myself in glowing terms six times over gives me a sort of spurious strength to go out about midnight and post them. If they all agree with Biddy Benson, I am as good as appointed already.

I have not had any replies to my letters. At first I feel deflated about this, but, as the days go by, I almost forget them in the rush of the daily disasters that beset most classes in the transition from the old-fashioned to the latest modes in teaching.

Since the Easter holidays this year we have heard little else in the staffroom but vulgar boasts about going away for Easter holidays. Apparently some teachers can afford to go away now twice a year instead of once as in the old days. They can do it without promotion too. Maybe if I am promoted to Cresswell I shall be able to move up into the select set.

Miss McMenamie and Miss Grott have been for a week to Scarborough and we are still hearing about it. But, mysteriously, they have been more distant to one another since coming back.

'It's better to go to a good hotel than just to a boarding house,' says Miss McMenamie.

'Were there many visitors?' asks Bella.

'The place was full,' says Miss Grott.

'Full of teachers, eh?' says Bella. 'Anyone can spot us a mile away.'

'Nobody guessed I was a teacher,' says Miss Grott.

'The two men you were always wanting to sit beside at the table – they did, first time,' says Miss McMenamie.

Miss Grott's face becomes suffused – whether with blushes or rage it is impossible to say.

'You mean I told them – when they asked what my job was. And,' she goes on, 'I don't think it's anything to be ashamed of.'

I feel Miss Grott and Miss McMenamie will be having no more holidays together. Miss Grott speaks airily of a 'cruise in the summer with my friend from Aberdeen'.

Bet comes up to me and whispers, 'Any word yet?'

'Not a cheep,' I say in a disillusioned tone. 'Never really expected any. I told you it would be a waste of time.'

'Not at all. Plenty of time yet. Think of being able to go to an hotel on the proceeds without anybody knowing you are a teacher.'

'They'd be misled by my joyous expression, I suppose.'

This morning I receive a reply from the Rev Horace Pickering, who invites me to his Rectory on Saturday morning. I show this triumph to Bet.

'Didn't I tell you?' she says.

'What shall I wear?'

'My brother wore his best suit. It was what you call a quiet suit.'

'Do you think I should wear my New Look? Or will it be too modern for the Reverend?'

'At least the coat will be decently half-way to your ankles. I think you could risk it.'

The New Look has crept but slowly into Scottish schools, almost as slowly as the new methods, which are regarded with strong suspicion. I have saved my clothing coupons by adding to my best coat a broad band of fur, thus lengthening it to the prevailing mode, as featured in the more advanced magazines. If it is a cold day on Saturday, I decide to wear it, for Broadlaw Moor sounds as cold as the high Himalaya.

I leave the school on Friday, thinking how drab, how war-stained and time-weary it looks. The old brown paint and varnish are cracking everywhere in post-war despair. No new looks here. I am glad to have at least the chance of leaving Garlock St. Cresswell is a much more modern school, built in 1936, whereas Garlock St was built in 1896. Continual demolition of old buildings all around it does nothing to attract new recruits to its staff.

As I leave, I feel my feet are set in the right direction – outward.

Saturday

I discover I have to change trains at Paisley in order to reach Broadlaw. There is only one train in two hours to this moorland retreat. I am wearing my home-improved coat, and I am thankful for the broad band of fur at the hem. I hope the moor will not be too windswept, as my hat feels rather insecure, due, I expect, to my lack of practice, for I seldom wear hats except on occasions of ceremony. I suppose going to a Rectory could be classed as going to a church. Hence the hat, which has an unstable feeling in spite of an elastic band at the back.

I am the only person, it seems, foolhardy enough to alight at Broadlaw Halt, for halt it seems to be rather than a station. Apart from the surprised ticket-collector, I am not the only one on the platform, for which I had to make a leap from the compartment. At the far end I see a strange figure which has an eighteenth-century outline. It comes towards me and I can hardly believe it. A short barrel-shaped man with a flat wide-brimmed hat, a flaring black coat to his knees – and gaiters – comes fussily forward.

'I am Horace Pickering.' He shakes my hand and removes his flat hat at the same time with a courtly sweep. 'You are the candidate, I presume.'

'Yes,' I say.

All he needs to complete the Johnsonian effect is a full-bottomed wig – oh, and buckles to his shoes. I observe these are thick with countryman soles. I look at my own war-utility court shoes, somewhat ill-adapted to the terrain.

'I shall escort you to the Rectory. It is a considerable distance. Communications here are infrequent. We are rather remote, you know.'

I see myself having to sleep the night in his cowshed. I set off at nine this morning, and it is already half past eleven.

'How kind of you to meet me,' I say, realizing that so far I have only uttered a solitary monosyllable.

'Do it for them all,' he says. 'You see, there's only one path. We're so much off the beaten track.'

There is, in fact, no beaten track, just a sort of sheep-run which goes over grass, on and on, and up and up, until my hat has shifted to an acute angle. The Rev Horace has clapped his hand on top of it twice to restrain its inclination to fly over Broadlaw. Conversation is not possible for me any more with the exertion. On we go, as we say in these parts, 'peching up the brae'.

A plantation of foolhardy trees stands near the top of the hill, all bunched together and veering from windward like a lot of drunks supporting one another home on a Saturday night. As it is, this is Saturday morning, and for me, one of the most askew.

The Rectory turns out to be right in the middle of this rampart of squint trees, and when we reach the centre the wind suddenly drops, and I am able to sweep the wisps of hair under my hat and contemplate a Victorian house in the usual compound of styles – fancy gables, a turret and little Gothic windows. Close to it is a dense shrubbery of laurels. Hacking our way through this by an overgrown path, we arrive at a ponderous oak door with a heavy knocker like a gargoyle.

The Rev Horace does not disturb this malevolent knocker, but pulls down an unpretentious iron handle at the side of the door. I hear no sound, but it must have had some effect, for in seconds a middle-aged maid in lace cap and apron opens the door.

Inside it is like a Brontë museum. I am given a chair upholstered in leather. I am glad I am not invited to sit on the other chair which has a forbidding horse-hair covering. But the one I am on has its own discomforts, for it slopes slightly towards the front. I have to exert some muscular pressure to avoid slipping slowly onto the worn Persian carpet. I cling to one of the arms. The Rev Horace installs himself behind a massive mahogany bureau.

'Now,' he says, adjusting a pair of gold-rimmed glasses, 'you are the candidate for Newark Park, you're at present in Gillespie Lane Primary, and I have your testimonial from the Head of St Kentigern's.'

'Oh no,' I say. 'I'm the candidate for Cresswell and I'm at present in Garlock St. My testimonial is from Bid – Miss Benson of Greeninch High.'

'Really! Ah – m'm.' He rifles through an immense untidy stack of papers on his desk. 'Garlock St, you say – yes – a school we are beginning to have trouble in staffing – Ah! here it is! Bedelia Benson, isn't it? I wonder if she's the same Bedelia Benson who was in my year at Edinburgh University. A Doctor of Divinity, isn't she?'

'Oh, no, she's a teacher of English in Greeninch High School.'

He looks keenly at the document he holds in his hand, one of my laborious midnight copies.

'She says you were a distinguished student at the University. Then she goes on to say something very contradictory. She says you gained a second prize – second only – in – eh, what's this? – Economics.'

'Yes,' I say.

'Now,' he says, removing his gold-rimmed glasses and using them to tap the testimonial. 'I don't think that makes you a distinguished student. No – definitely – not for only a second prize.'

I forbear to tell him that it was won in the field of battle from a hundred and seventy other students, four-fifths of whom were men!

He goes on. 'Your Miss Bedelia Benson has just a hint of exaggeration in her use of epithets. Obviously, a second cannot be regarded as distinguished, not nearly distinguished enough –'

'I'll not be teaching Economics to infants. Maybe Miss Benson has been emphasizing the wrong things – just trying to help, as it were –'

I flounder on. He shakes his head again and puts on his glasses.

'Would you like a glass of port?'

By this time I feel as small as the man in the old advertisement who had never heard of Worthington. I could cheerfully have drowned my embarrassment in a whole butt of Malmsey.

He pulls an enamelled bell-handle at the side of the fireplace, and the lace cap and apron brings in a massive silver tray with a huge decanter and what looks like two matching tankards upon it. Horace pours a generous measure into both glasses and offers me one. I feel this is rather overdoing the consolation and think of the narrowness of that sheep-run going down the hill. Commendably, I remember not to say 'Cheers!' when I raise the tankard.

I sip. The Rev Horace sips. The port is what you might call full-bodied.

'Tell me what you are interested in teaching,' he says, suddenly emerging into the twentieth century.

I recount my cherished theories and expound the new methods as lucidly as I can, with limited sips at the port. I stress the need for having young teachers – not too young, of course – in promoted posts, especially in Infant promoted posts, where agility is needed with all these new gymnastics being introduced. Yes, I say, to skip around a Gym hall you must be mimble – sorry, nimble – (port talking) –

'What other subjects have you studied? Tell me about your Greek and Latin.'

'Well – eh – you see, I don't think I'm ever likely to be teaching Greek and Latin to six or even seven-year-olds.'

'I learned Greek and Latin at the age of seven.'

'We don't do that nowadays.' I think of the Garlock St mob struggling to learn the English language.

'My train leaves at one o'clock, I think,' I say tentatively. This interview could go on for another hour if the next item to be discussed is mathematics for midgets. I am already condemned by the whole interview.

'I am not forgetting your train,' he says, rising. I put my glass back on the mighty salver, hoping he does not notice I have only absorbed half.

'I shall escort you back to the station.'

'I think I know the way back,' I say, but when I rise I am less sure. I am weaving slightly as we go out. 'Please don't bother to come.'

'I escort all the ladies, I assure you.'

The winds of Broadlaw contrive to mitigate the sensation of swimming down the sheep-run, and we reach the platform at the station just as a whistle announces a voluptuous plume of steam from a locomotive which trails disproportionately only one carriage behind it. One woman descends from it. I hastily try to step up into it, and am thankful the New Look is wide enough. The step was built for more aloof station platforms than this, and I am assisted by a mighty push from the Rev Horace.

'Goodbye,' he says from below. 'I still think, you know, that a second is not distinguished enough – '

I look out of the window and see him doffing his clerical

sombrero and going over to shake hands with the woman who has descended from the train wearing a dated 1936 costume.

I have a feeling she is the one for Newark Park, is at present in Gillespie Lane Primary, and has a testimonial from the Head of St Kentigern's.

May
1947

On Monday morning everyone stops talking when I enter the staffroom.

'I know whom you are talking about,' I say to the silence.

'How did you get on at the interview?' asks Bet eagerly.

'I'm quite sure I didn't get on at all. I'm afraid I made no impression.'

'Tell me,' says Bella, 'did you get a glass of port?'

'Yes!' I say. 'How did you know?'

'Interviews with the Rev Horace follow a pattern. Did he meet you and see you off at the station?'

'That's right. It was all rather surprising.'

'Any more answers to any more letters?' asks Bet.

'Not so far,' I say.

'I disagree absolutely with canvassing,' sniffs Miss Grott. 'It should be declared illegal. That – and what they call "influence".'

'If the weapons are swords,' says Bet, 'it's no use retaliating with boxing gloves.'

Miss Grott pats her latest perm. 'It should be merit,' she says.

'You should apply then,' says Bet, 'provided, of course, that you can produce the merit certificate.'

We all know that Miss Grott has never studied for the special certificate. But the ringing of the bell terminates further acrimonies.

Bet pursues me into my classroom.

'Do you think you made a good impression? Did he think you had a wonderful testimonial?'

'Far from it. According to him, Bedelia wrote a fiction yarn right enough. My poor miserable second prize was not distinguished enough. I am definitely not on that short list.'

But I am!

And this after I have been interviewed by yet another member of Committee, a rabid Labour Councillor, who lives in a council house and has Attlee's portrait over the mantelpiece in the living-room beside two 'Presents from Rothesay' in the form of china mugs. He asks questions about Keir Hardie and Ernest Bevin instead of about the Look-Say or the Sentence Method – or Greek or Latin. He has an intense interest in school meals and thinks canteens are the best form of messes for the masses. I leave him with about the same degree of disillusion as I left the Rev Horace.

The Head sends for me about ten o'clock and, with a hurt expression warring with condemnation of plotting behind his back, shows me a letter inviting me to appear at an interview at County Headquarters on the last Thursday of this month.

The last Thursday in May, 1947

I go to school again in my coat with the fur surround, the temperature being about 32°F this morning. After all, only two members of the Committee have ever seen me in it. I am also saving my clothing coupons for the summer holidays. I am to leave the school at ten to catch the train.

Bella has heard that there are five teachers on the short list for Cresswell School. There is intense interest in all the short lists, as which Head you land with determines your happiness or misery for years. Now that I am on one myself, I am avid for information which will help me to withstand the ordeal.

'You haven't a chance,' says Bella. 'If there's anybody who's been an Infants Mistress already, she'll be the one.'

'How do we ever get new ones, then?' asks Bet. Bella ignores this logicality.

'The woman from Gardiner St – a Miss McKenzie – is almost sure to get it,' she says. 'You'll never get the job, for you're too young if you're under forty. I can't think why they ever put you on the list.'

'Good luck, anyway,' says Bet. 'Although you just might regret applying when you stand up to make that speech to all the members of Committee. That was the only bit that stuck my brother.'

'Speech!' I say in consternation. 'You didn't tell me I should have to make a speech!'

'Well, you do,' puts in Miss McMenamie. 'It's gruelling too. So I've heard. I for one would never have the cheek to stand up in front of all those men – on a platform.'

She speaks with horror in her voice as if it were a striptease act.

'Platform!' I echo. This is worse and worse. Why didn't Bet tell me all? I feel like running along to the Head's room and withdrawing my application.

'Oh,' says Bet, 'you'll get on all right. Make up the speech in the train.'

'They'll ask you which church you go to,' says Miss Grott as a parting encouragement. 'Religious discrimination, I call it.'

I go to my class, but I am little able to concentrate this morning on collecting the milk and dinner money. There is a long line of children for meals today. I cannot understand why the meals are so popular all of a sudden. That would happen on a crisis morning for me.

We have no dining-hall inside the school, and we are not permitted to use the Gym hall for eating in. Thus a compromise has been reached. We begin this week going in long lines to a building five minutes' walk from the school. Somebody had the diabolic idea of using this building, which has lain empty during and after the War. It is the hollow shell of what was to have been a mammoth picture palace called *The Silver Comet*. It has no real floor, just a strew of ashes, and the collapsible tables are set uncertainly upon this. All around are skeleton girders which look as if they have just walked in from the shipyards across the road. Blasts of cold air rush in from time to time for none of the rickety doors fit. It is like a refugee camp in Eastern Europe. Mince, turnip and potatoes appear with dreary regularity. Plum duff worthy of the 1914–18 War follows monotonously and is called 'desert', according to the compositions on 'My First School Meal' produced by Primaries Six and Seven.

Today I shall escape the duty at this canteen. Yesterday I was hot on the track of the Red Indian who had left a trail of plum duff between *The Silver Comet* and the school. Plum duff to follow indeed! Although I followed the spoor determinedly, I never caught up with the culprit. Does the Education Committee ever know what goes on? I am so annoyed about the whole idea of *The Silver Comet* that I find myself composing a fiery speech about it to deliver on that platform.

Paul Klimasiefski, an engaging young Pole who came in with the war waifs, is standing at my elbow watching as finally I gather all the money for the dinners together and check it. He continues to watch as I put it in the cash bag, close the Milk and Dinner books, lock the desk and pick up my keys. It is five minutes to ten, and I feel tension mounting. I pop my head round Bet's door and give her my keys. She is to supervise my class while I am gone – and her own as well, of course.

'They're all yours now,' I say gleefully.

I am just leaving when suddenly I wonder what Paul wants, standing so patiently at my desk.

'Well – what is it?' I say.

'It's to give you my dinner money for the "Silver Comic",' he says. I ignore his money.

'You can starve!' I say heartlessly and fly to the staffroom for my hat. Then I fly to the station and just manage to catch the train by half a minute. The hat is dislodged considerably by this time, although it has been in worse places, such as Broadlaw Moor. I wonder if the Rev Horace will be at the interview – oh, and the Rev McGowan – and, without doubt, the Labour Councillor who likes messing about in canteens. I may not be among strangers after all.

Having set my hat straight in the station waiting-room, I make my way to the Education Offices. I have not yet begun to breathe normally and my pulse rate increases in inverse ratio to my nearness to them. It is a cold morning, with the arctic air of the early frosts that sometimes breathe upon Scotland in the merry month. But I am heated by apprehension, increasing doubt, and alarm at the unknown.

As I enter the Education Offices, a scorching blast of equatorial air meets me, such as I have never experienced in any school. I am conducted by a fashionably-coiffured, nylon-stockinged and faultlessly-tailored secretary holding a sheaf of papers, and find myself delivered to a cosy room full of well-upholstered furniture where sit four unknown women. They all stop talking and there is an uncomfortable silence.

I tentatively take the only vacant chair, an upright model such as is prescribed for staffrooms, except that this one is new and has a padded seat. The other four over-stuffed chairs are already occupied by the earlier candidates trying out luxuries they have never had in their schools. The heat is overpowering.

'That's the lot now,' says one of the women. Nobody smiles. Cut-throat competition.

I notice that they all wear 1936 tweed costumes and felt hats in a range of unpleasing shades. They all carry umbrellas, and one of them subscribes to style by having a dated silver fox fur draped over her shoulder as in the fashion of 1936. She keeps this on all the time in spite of the heat. Prestige value. They scrutinize my New Look coat, it seems to me without approval.

'Five is too many,' says the woman with the fur.

'Can't think why they needed five,' says the one sitting next to her.

I feel that I am the extra woman.

As I look at the four faces, I recognize one of them as belonging to a teacher who taught me as a pupil in the Primary when I was a child in Greeninch. I remember how I idolized her too. So I smile delightedly and say,

'Why! Surely it's Miss McKenzie! Don't you remember me? You taught me in Greeninch years ago, in the Infant department. I was in your class – '

She turns a hard and rejectful eye upon me. The others look at me in amazement.

'And you weren't the best of them,' she says sniffily. Obviously I have made a serious blunder in daring to be on the same short list as my old teacher.

'There should be an age limit,' says one of the others, 'but there's no doubt about who gets appointed – the one with the long experience every time. None of us have anything to fear there.'

Clearly I have everything to fear. If the worst comes to the worst and my miserable eighteen years are actually considered enough for me ever to be appointed, then I can expect mayhem. If I am not appointed, then for them God's still in his Heaven. I wish I had never applied for promotion. It is true what Bella said. Anyone who succeeds at my age will be something of a professional oddity. I almost run out and leave them to their unchallenged triumph. At that moment the smartly-dressed secretary appears again, making them all look drab, dreary and démodé. This gives me a malicious satisfaction.

'Miss McKenzie first,' she says.

While Miss McKenzie goes to the inquisition, I am left with the other three, and there is an uneasy silence.

In a surprisingly short space of time, Miss McKenzie returns, and 'Miss McSween' is called out. The remaining two pounce on Miss McKenzie.

'What did they ask you?'

'There's no reason to suppose that they'll ask you the same.'

23

'Tell us anyway.'

'They asked about – these modern ideas.'

'Really?'

'I didn't know much about them. I just told them that the old ones were good enough for me.'

'Good for you! – But I don't know much about them either.'

'Did they ask you if you were a Sunday School teacher?'

'Not a word about that – and I am.'

'How many were there?'

'Nearly the whole Committee – over thirty.'

'Who's the Chairman?'

'The Rev Horace Pickering.'

'Oh, dear, he's so absent-minded.'

Miss McSween comes back, and is very red in the face. Before I can learn what they asked her, I myself am called. The secretary opens a door at the end of the carpeted corridor and announces me.

'In you go,' she says encouragingly, when I teeter on the threshold.

I am aware of the heat getting worse. If only I could trap some of it for use next winter in Garlock St. Yes, I'm sure I'll be back there next winter.

I step forward and feel isolated in the middle of a spacious room full of carpet. 'A don from the dais serene' speaks my name –

'Come right forward to the platform.'

It's true! There is a platform! I step up onto it. I am aware of the Rev Horace seated between the Labour Councillor and an unknown man on my right-hand side. A triumvirate of terror.

'Now tell the members about your work.'

I stand at first dumb, and turn to face the jury. They sit on the remaining three sides of the square with an acreage of carpet in the middle. I see no comforting familiar face. Just imagine, I say to myself, that it's Primary One. After a preliminary squeak, I explain my work and what I should like to do to improve it. Then all of a sudden I am saying what it is that keeps me from doing it, the time spent in writing up forms, interruptions, unstable timetables, increasing Gym without facilities, shivering in classrooms and walking to unattractive school meals in unattractive places. I suddenly stop, appalled. The resulting anticlimax is that there seems to be no violent reaction.

'You are not pleased with the school meals, you say?' This from a man with a bald head and pebble glasses who sits near the platform. 'I understood that these were wholesome – very wholesome, considering the food situation at present.' He speaks in a voice almost in the range of a bat. I want to laugh at the peculiar noise it is.

'It's more the conditions under which they eat –' I tail off.

'The children nevertheless eat them, regardless –'

'Oh no,' I say, 'yesterday they left the pudding in the street.' This time I call forth a shocked silence.

'You have only eighteen years' experience.' This from the Rev Horace.

'You can learn to teach pretty well in a lot less,' I say, now warmed up with eloquence.

'That will be all.'

I stand for a moment rather dazed, feeling a little like the day of the port up at Broadlaw. Then I come to, and hurriedly descend from the platform and walk across the expanse of carpet, feeling like a beetle crossing a ten-acre field.

I arrive back in the ante-room and the next victim goes to the execution.

'What did they ask you?'

Suddenly I am of the hierarchy, having now been fully blooded.

'I can't remember any questions. I was asked to condemn myself out of my own mouth.'

'Oh, really?'

'I wish I'd never come. I'll not be appointed, that's certain. You are all so experienced.'

'I've been at it thirty-two years,' says Miss McSween.

'And I,' says Miss McKenzie, trumping her ace, 'have been thirty-six.'

'I'm sure you'll be appointed, Euphemia,' says Miss McSween. 'I should never, never go onto short lists for interviews. It makes my high blood pressure worse. My doctor warned me against it.'

'How many have you been on?' I ask, greatly impressed.

'At least twelve, I think. But I suffer for it every time. Nervous prostration, you know.'

'Don't worry, Caroline,' says Miss McKenzie. 'It's all over now and we'll look forward to a nice lunch in Berteloni's. They're open again. Closed during the War.'

'Yes,' says the remaining woman, whose name I do not know, and who can hardly be feeling like lunch, as her ordeal is still to come. 'And it's nice to know that the Education Committee will be paying for it too.'

'Paying for it!' I exclaim.

'Oh, yes,' says Miss McKenzie. 'Don't forget to claim your lunch money and your train fare at the office on the way out.'

'When do we know who's been appointed?' I ask.

'If you know anybody on the Committee you could hang around until they come out – and maybe somebody will give you a hint.'

'Oh, I could never do that. I'd blush for shame.'

'It's a pity', says Miss McKenzie, 'that there's only one short list today. When there are three or four for Headmasters it's a lot cheerier.'

'The men are so good at lobbying,' says Miss McSween. 'They fight to the death, too – '

I leave as the secretary calls out 'Miss Young'.

I discover I am very hungry, and so I go to claim my expenses. A clerk, who is better dressed than any of the Headmasters I know, hands me the money over the counter. I am suffering from the reaction, and I'm sure I look battered and that my hat is again at a drunken angle.

The clerk says, 'Treat yourself to a brandy as well, hen.'

I smile faintly and pocket the money. I decide to try and find the recommended *cordon bleu* place mentioned by Miss McKenzie. It turns out to be a smart restaurant, much to be preferred to *The Silver Comet*. I shall chalk everything up to experience and regard this as a day out.

Thus it is that I am half-way through a plate of – yes – mince, turnip and potatoes, when three of the other four candidates come in.

'Miss Young got it!' bursts out Miss McSween. 'And she was so excited that she dashed off to buy a new hat.'

Miss McKenzie is looking glum and dispirited. I feel for her, but, after all, she is an Infants Mistress already. This post would only have boosted her salary by £20 per annum, whereas to me it would have meant that now-evaporated £65. Everybody is at last out of her misery, except perhaps Miss McKenzie. My presence also has not made her day a success.

'Let's see,' she says, lifting the menu. 'We'll make the best of it, and have – ah! grilled sole – '

'I'll have the cheese dish,' says Miss McSween. 'I don't know how Berteloni's manages to have all this variety.'

The waitress comes along. The sole is off, she says. So is the cheese dish.

I think how at this moment the Garlock St mob is tucking in at Paul Klimasiefski's 'Silver Comic'.

'Just mince, turnip and potatoes left,' says the waitress. 'And plum duff to follow.'

'No obvious scars of battle,' says Bet Dodd, after I have answered the spate of questions which descends upon me this morning.

'The scars I have don't show,' I say.

'I'd never be able to face a whole Committee,' says Miss McCondrick. 'I'd be in a state of nerves and have to be given sedatives. I can sympathize with that Miss McSween you told us about. Of course, I'm not desperate for promotion.'

'I'm not desperate either,' I say. 'Partly curious – partly avaricious.'

'I was sure you'd never have a chance,' says Miss Grott. 'You'll have to wait until you're fifty-five at least, and it might just begin to be possible.'

'I might even be dead by then.'

'And', she goes on, 'maybe by that time all this nonsense of

27

canvassing and lying in wait in lobbies will have been outlawed.'

'I'm damned if I'll wait until I'm a crabbed crone,' I say, fighting-confident now that I am on the outside of the carpeted room. The ordeal is transmuted by the passage of the hours into a dramatic tale to tell to the uninitiated. I am in the rare position of being the only woman in Garlock St who has entered the lion's den and come back to boast.

'One thing more,' I say, donning a turtle-necked sweater before descending to my classroom in the Polar ice-cap, and putting on my overall on top of that, 'if you ever do pay a visit to the Education Offices, you'll be met and welcomed at the door – by lovely torrid air from Central Africa.'

April
1950

I am again a candidate for promotion, a decent interval having expired since my first debut in the lists – although according to some, the interval is not decent enough.

I find when I reach the still super-heated Education building that this time all the candidates are about my own age. Have the decrepit ladies all been used up by the abrasions of applying for posts? It is either that, or the smallness of the school where the vacancy is. It has, of course, a correspondingly small responsibility payment – £35 per annum and only two teachers to boss.

The school I have applied for this time is Heatherbrae, about a mile up the hill from Garlock St, and, although older than Garlock St, yet with a tradition behind it and country airs around it. It is surrounded by the villas on the extreme west of the town. Unfortunately for the owners of the villas, the extreme east of Greeninch, a district called Homeston, is cheek by jowl with it.

Here east meets west and the twain both meet and clash, for Greeninch is building one of its housing schemes just there.

I know most of the answers to most of the questions this time. Miss Grott's ideal recipe for promotion has been realized. I write no letters. I am given no prior interviews. I need no testimonial. The Education Offices have got us all taped. It is as dreary as a station waiting-room and as colourless as the Labour Exchange. The drama, the buskined actors and the emotive platform are gone. No triumvirate sits over a dignified senate.

I sit at one end of a board-room table, and face a Committee of six. I am there no more than four minutes. I am already all written down in carbon copies lying on the table before each member. One is a woman, and she is even less exciting than Miss McKenzie or Miss McSween. It is just like Miss Grott to have conceived of such a thing as this.

No one is given a hint as to who has been appointed. Lobbying has gone out of favour – and out of flavour too.

'Who got it?' I am besieged in the staffroom this morning.

'I have no idea,' I say.

A week elapses. Still no revelation. The retiring Infants Mistress up at Heatherbrae takes her presentation easy chair and departs. The staff of Garlock St say they will not envy me if I am her successor, as nobody up there can tolerate the Headmaster, noted as he is himself for intolerance.

I am waiting at the bus stop after school this afternoon when Mrs McDade, carrying a loaded shopping basket in each hand, joins me in the queue. She has had seven red-haired children in Garlock St in the past and is now Granny to one who is in my present class.

'I hear ye're leavin' the school,' she says resentfully. 'Goin' up to that snob school at Heatherbrae.'

'Am I?' I say.

'Aye,' she goes on. 'Don't deny it. They say ye're gettin' promoted.'

Her tone implies extreme disapproval. I am obviously leaving her grandson Jamie shamefully in the lurch by even thinking of moving out of Garlock St. It reveals to me what a corner-stone I seem to have become.

'Who told you this?' I ask, very curious.

'Who d'ye think?' she says. 'Wee Jamie came home at dinner-time wi' the news.'

And that was the way they brought the good news from Jamie to me.

I receive a letter today corroborating Jamie's prediction. I have been appointed as Infants Mistress at Heatherbrae and will report there on a date to be intimated later. If I agree to accept this appointment, will I sign below. I immediately grab a pen and sign. But I puzzle forever as to how Jamie McDade found out yesterday. Children are becoming more precocious, I am told. Well, the McDades could do with plenty more of that.

Miss McCondrick makes a prediction too – of an unhappy future for me.

'The Boss up there is terrible,' she says. 'He only kept his staff because up till now jobs were scarce. But wait – wait till a few more years have passed and all the post-war children come flooding in.'

'Some of the Staff at Heatherbrae have applied for transfers this year,' says Miss McMenamie. 'I know at least four who did that at Easter. They want to be moved next term.'

'And,' says Miss Grott, 'maybe only one will ever get a transfer.'

'But four!' I say. 'That's nearly half of the whole Staff. There are only ten altogether. I hope none of the Infant Staff applied.'

'Oh, no, they're only probationers.'

'Fresh minds – young ideas,' I say to this implied criticism.

'I heard last week,' says Bella, 'that the Head of Heatherbrae was in hospital over the Easter holidays.'

'Really?' says Miss McCondrick, sounding as if he had succeeded where she had failed. 'I was never told that, and as you know, I've been in and out of hospital myself several times during the past year.'

'It's quite true,' says Bella.

'It'll maybe chasten him a bit,' says the heartless Miss Mc-Menamie.

'Or make him more girny than ever,' says Miss Grott. 'I once taught in a school where he was First Assistant and he overruled everything the Headmaster wanted to do.' She turns to me.

'You'll maybe regret having gone to all that trouble to get promotion.'

'What trouble?' I say lightly. 'No trouble now. No canvassing, no nothing. All mechanical, without human feeling. They did it your way this time.'

I decide today to have a flitting. I shall transport some of my accumulated teaching materials up to Heatherbrae, so that I shall not have it all to do when I finally leave Garlock St. But there is such a great deal of material – my personal books, handwork scrap, music books, models – that I ask Alex Purdie, our First Assistant, if he can supply me with some beasts of burden from Primary Seven. At 3.15 pm he sends me three stalwarts, more reputed for brawn than brain, who gleefully shoulder the stores, as being more in their line than decimal fractions.

Heatherbrae is a cut above Garlock St for several reasons. It is two hundred feet above for one thing, and the other thing is that it has a flagpole. This flagpole has long been a status symbol, conferred upon the school by a ship-builder who thought he owed his millions to the schooling he had in it when he was a boy. This is a most stimulating idea. Seems to have gone out of fashion.

The flagpole comes into view foot by foot as our procession winds up Rosetree Avenue. It occurs to me to wonder on what important occasions the flag would be hoisted. Wryly I think, 'After all the trouble I have had getting here, it ought to be hoisted for me.'

I raise my eyes and it would seem I have the second sight – for behold! I see the flag fluttering up the mast, its device as yet undecipherable. It reaches the top and bravely unfurls its folds in the breeze. I am touched by emotion. What a gracious gesture for a new Infants Mistress! Garlock St has nothing on Heatherbrae for good manners. The boys ahead of me call out:

'They're pitten up the flag, miss! Is it for us?'

'It could be,' I say modestly.

We turn in at the school gates. We have still to negotiate the wide impressive flight of steps that leads into the front playground, between two cherry trees in bloom. I am going to like being in Heatherbrae with its nearness to nature.

The janitor is busy with the ropes at the flagpole. And, just as we begin to cross the playground, down comes the flag again. The janitor adjusts it at half-mast and hastily scuttles round the back of the school and disappears, as one who deals an insult and is ashamed. And I am deeply insulted. His timing has been nicely calculated to slap me in the face.

'Whit's he leavin' it like that for?' says Ernie Forrest, setting down his two cardboard cartons on the front steps at the east door.

'It's at hauf-mast,' says Jim McAllister.

'Whit's that for?' asks Jackie Paterson.

'Ye're an ignorant lot,' says Ernie. 'It means somebody's deid.'

I meet the janitor now emerging by the east door. He has a large brass bell in his hand.

'We're from Garlock St,' I say. 'I'm the new Infants Mistress. Perhaps we could dump our stuff somewhere. Then I'd like to see the Headmaster.'

'Ye'll no' dae that the day,' he says, and places the bell on a ledge behind the door. 'I'm no' tae ring the bell the day.'

'Really!' I say, beginning to be suspicious of momentous things. 'Why did you lower the flag as we came in?'

'As a mark o' respec',' he says. 'The Heidmaister died at dinner-time.'

'There!' says Ernie. 'I tell't ye all. I wish Garlock St had a flag. Then we could pit it up and doon noo and then.'

Apparently the school are to file out, silently and without benefit of bell, as a further mark of respect. They do this while we wait at the front door. Then we go in and dump our burdens in the corridor, and the Garlock St boys are dismissed – a whole quarter of an hour earlier than usual and much to their liking. I obtain the keys and open a cupboard in the corridor where the janitor says 'she' (I suppose he means the last Infants Mistress) kept her 'things'.

I expect to see complete sets of equipment. But the cupboard is as bare as Mother Hubbard's. There is a lonely box containing coloured sticks which look as if they had been sucked rather than handled, and a box of plasticine still in its grease-proof wrapper.

It takes me half an hour to stow away all my materials in the cupboard and by that time it is full. I hope the cupboards in the classrooms are more capacious.

As I leave, the flag with its indeterminate device is rolling droopily half-way down the flagpole. I wonder what the successor to the deceased Head of Heatherbrae will be like, and if they will put the flag up to the top for him.

The Staff at Garlock St are sitting as usual in a ring round the fire, now permitted in the month of May. All are talking at once when I come in.

'Is it true', they all say, 'about the Head of Heatherbrae?'

'It is,' I say.

'Aren't you lucky!' says Miss Grott, as if she regretted it.

'Maybe I'll get worse,' I say. 'At any rate, I've got a lot of my stuff up there now. And I needed it too. Bare as a desert. I'll have plenty of time now to shift the rest during next month.'

'Have you any word when you're to leave here?' asks Bet.

'I expect I'll not have to take up the post until next term,' I say.

As I am on my way to the classroom, I am waylaid by the Head.

'I have a letter for you,' he says. 'Come to my room.'

'Apparently you are to report to Heatherbrae tomorrow morning,' he says. He hands me the letter, which has obviously been an enclosure in one of his, telling him he is to lose a teacher immediately.

'Very inconvenient,' he says. He does not say for whom, but it's obviously not for me.

I stay behind until five o'clock tonight and stack the remaining boxes at the back of the classroom. Although I have paid one visit to Heatherbrae, I do not know my way around up there, nor where anything is kept, nor any of the Staff.

I suffer a delayed shattering of nerves, and for once sympathize with Miss McCondrick. In fact, I could do with one of her pills.

This morning I climb up the hill to Heatherbrae. I am puffing with exertion and apprehension coming up the road, which is a rough path in keeping with the bucolic nature of this outlying part of the town. I reach the school and for a moment feel a sense of satisfaction in passing through its portals. It is a single-storey building of good grey stone, with gracious lines, elegant, and at the same time more homely than Garlock St. The grassy slopes on either side of the front steps give an air of collegiate grandeur to it, as do its two sets of Gothic windows facing the front. There is an old belfry between the two sets of windows, but the janitor's hand-bell seems to have superseded the bell that hangs there. Maybe the rope which such an old bell must have had, was an overpowering temptation to the kids. I'm sure I'd have tugged it myself.

The flag still droops half-way down the mast. It is appropriate for me today. I feel at half-mast myself.

I go in and at the end of a short corridor I see a door marked 'Headmaster'. I hesitate to knock on it as I would hesitate to knock on St Peter's gate, there being a quality of the sacrilegious in such an action, considering the demise of him who occupied it.

As I stand in this respectful uncertainty, the door is violently thrown open and a boy falls into my unready arms.

'Don't you come to me about your lost pants! I'm busy! Beat it!'

The door bangs in my face. The boy beats it. I knock tentatively after a decent interval has elapsed for the pot to have gone off the boil. The door is thrown open again.

'Didn't I say to beat it? – Oh! – I don't mean you. It was that boy. What is it anyway! I've very little time this morning –'

'That's why I've been sent,' I say. 'I'm the new Infants Mistress.'

His look is compounded of embarrassment and relief.

'Come in, come in,' he says, melting rapidly. 'You know how it is, having to take over at short notice – '

'I should know,' I say feelingly.

'The Head died suddenly the day before yesterday.'

'Yes,' I say. 'I came up with some things of mine. The school was dismissing, but I saw no teachers after that.'

'Oh, we're always in a hurry,' he says. 'So many things to attend to.'

I wonder. The things to attend to seem to be all outside the school. Some schools are like that. The moment the last bell of the day goes, everybody disappears by magic. Some lie in wait behind classroom doors waiting for the moment, in order to be the first to move the class out. It becomes a technique.

'By the way,' he says at last. 'I'm Fairlie Brown, the First Assistant.'

'I gathered that.'

'I'm thankful to see you,' he says.

'Not when I appeared outside your door just now the first time it opened. You didn't see me at all then.'

'No. That awful boy. Always coming bothering you when there's a crisis. And would you believe it, I hardly know the ropes here at all.'

'Really! I was hoping you'd – '

'It's all very complicated,' he says, knitting his brows, 'very complicated – Old Gregg – sorry – Mr Gregg – Gregory's Mixture, as he was called, you know – '

'No, I didn't know,' I say.

'He wouldn't let anybody do any of his work. Wouldn't delegate. Never left the school till six every night.'

So there was an exception to the on-the-bell brigade. But maybe that began on the very day he died.

'Never let me have a chance to be a real First Assistant,' goes on Fairlie Brown.

'Now's your chance,' I say. 'I've never had a chance to be an Infants Mistress. So we're in it together.'

'I'll take you along and introduce you to the Staff.'

We proceed along a corridor which seems to pass between the two wings, and emerge at the far end where we pass classrooms. The doors in this part are solid wooden doors, unlike those in the corridor which have glass panels. The silence is absolute.

We turn into a small cloakroom where there is a wash-basin and a woman bending over it.

'Ah! Here's Miss Brown,' he says. 'I was hoping you would be free just now.'

Miss Brown turns round. 'I'm not free,' she says, 'and I never am. I'm rinsing out Grace McKinnon's socks. She fell in a puddle outside the gate this morning.'

'Ah!' says Fairlie Brown. 'Always complications. Now, Miss Brown, maybe you would see that our new Infants Mistress is introduced to the rest of the ladies.'

I shake hands with Miss Brown after she has dried hers.

'I must go,' says Fairlie Brown, backing away. 'You came most opportunely,' he says to me, in a manner suggesting his escape. 'You see, I've to leave this morning at half-past ten for the Head's funeral. He lived outside of Glasgow, so it's hardly likely I'll be back at school today. That means, of course, that as you are now the next in command, you'll be in charge of the whole school.'

And before I can recover from this, he goes, with an expression of delight entirely inappropriate to a funeral.

It is a colourful Staff whom I meet later on. Including myself, there are eight women crowded into the few square yards of space comprising the smallest staffroom I have even seen. It also miraculously holds a bulky cupboard and a kitchen table. The colourfulness begins in their names, for there is a Miss Brown, a Miss Greene, a Miss Black and a Mrs Whyte (with a 'y', please). Miss Brown does all the explaining. She is a vivacious woman, maybe thirty years of age, tall and plump, and the vivacity is engendered in her remarkable brown eyes which, when combined with fair hair, always command a second look anywhere.

'I'm called Vera,' she says. 'Now, don't say the obvious. I know I'm supposed to be very brown, while he is only fairly brown!

That's an already outworn joke. What I do object to, and which is a grimmer joke, is that the kids think I'm Mrs Brown, his wife.'

She goes on with the introductions. 'This is Mrs Whyte – Daphne Whyte.'

I shake hands with this woman, who is the nearest to me. She is a very strange-looking woman, her most outstanding characteristic being her face, which appears to be powdered with blackboard chalk. Lank red hair hanging down her cheeks gives it a very bizarre effect. Her figure is floppy, and her voice has an edge to it, not uncommon in middle-aged teachers. Mrs Whyte I judge to be moving reluctantly to the end of her fifth decade.

'Miss Greene and Miss Black – Shirley and Marjorie,' goes on Vera, taking them in the order in which I can manage to reach their hands. 'They're your Infant Staff, both probationers, but hoping soon for Inspectors to license them.'

Shirley and Marjorie stretch over and shake hands.

'We're not really hoping for Inspectors all that much,' says Marjorie. 'You needn't worry. It won't happen on your first day. We've nearly completed our two years, so we're not just fledglings.'

Both are attractive girls, Shirley tall and dark-haired, Marjorie tall and fair-haired. I am pleased to have young staff.

'Shirley and Marjorie hope you'll not be too old-fashioned about the writing,' goes on the outspoken Vera. 'They're disgusted working with slates.'

'I spit on slates! Metaphorically, of course,' I say. 'As a matter of fact, I've never used slates for years. I hope you have plentiful supplies of sandstone blocks. I usually teach hieroglyphics on slabs, using chisels.'

Shirley and Marjorie giggle flatteringly, and look relieved.

'These two,' says Vera, indicating two women, maybe in the thirty-to-forty age range, 'are Rita McGarvey and Rena Steele.'

Both are petite women, remarkably alike, and dressed in clothes without an inch of slack to spare. This gives them an even more petite look with their neat, well-moulded figures and tiny high-heeled shoes. Both are creating a staffroom fug by vigorously puffing at cigarettes.

'We call them the Lums,' says Vera. 'They live round in the room-and-kitchen, and Rena has just broken off her engagement. You can still see the mark where the ring was.'

Neither Rita nor Rena seems to object to this highly-seasoned introduction.

'Room-and-kitchen?' I say.

'Two classrooms,' explains Vera. 'We call it the "room-and-kitchen" – or the but-and-ben if you are pro-Scottish. It's really an annexe built on at the back of the school.'

'I'm in the kitchen bit,' says Rita. 'And it has a cooker in it. War surplus. Rena has a sink in her room.'

'Jolly useful, that sink,' says Rena. 'All rooms in schools should have sinks, but white, not black, like mine.'

'The cooker takes up a lot of room,' says Rita. 'There's not an inch of space left. Something like this staffroom. Pardon me standing on your feet, Rena.'

'You certainly seem crowded in here,' I say. 'But you'll be one less when I go to my private room. Will one of you show me where it is?'

'Private room!' they all exclaim together.

'I'm afraid you've been sold ideas of opulence,' says Vera. 'Did you apply for this job really thinking you'd get a room of your own?'

'I didn't think of it till now. I took it for granted.'

'In this school the Infants Mistress pigs it in here with us,' says Vera.

'As long as nobody objects, I don't mind a bit. But – it won't give you much scope for talking about me behind my back.'

'I see you understand one of the functions of head teachers,' says Rita.

'By the way,' says Vera, opening a door in a corner. 'This is the WC and wash-up. Sorry no hot water though – but there's a sink in your classroom which occasionally agrees to produce some.'

'And,' says Rita, 'the last Infants Mistress used this WC as a changing-room when she was going on a spree straight from school. None of us could get in for ages. Then she'd issue forth in her velvet and sequins.'

'And,' says Daphne Whyte, who so far has been looking me over, 'another teacher, who shall be nameless, used to tie her West Highland terrier up in it, until one day the Head came along here with the Chief Psychologist and it barked.'

'Extraordinary!' I say.

'I hope you haven't a dog,' says Rena.

'No,' I say, 'nor a gown of velvet and sequins either.' At that moment an older lady who so far has not been presented to me pipes up.

'Nobody has introduced me to our new Infants Mistress.'

'Oh, sorry,' says Vera. 'You're so retiring, Ailie.' And I am introduced to Ailie Chapman, the oldest member of the Staff, who teaches Primary Six, or, as she calls it, the Sub Qualy.

'I see that none of you here wear overalls,' I say.

'Gave it over during the War to save coupons for dresses,' says Rena.

'Is this a dirty school?' I ask. 'Garlock St was, especially during the War. Had to scatter Keating's Powder over the floor below my desk. Fleas every day.'

'So far we have no complaints on that score,' says Vera. 'And don't ever let old Gurney hear any criticisms of his floors.'

'Who's old Gurney?'

'The janitor. Gurney by name and girny by nature,' says Daphne.

'I must make closer acquaintance with him soon,' I say. 'As a matter of policy, I like to make a friend of the janitor. Always better to be for him than against him.'

'Nobody can be *for* our Gurney. Everybody's against,' says Daphne Whyte.

This is bad news. This, and no private room to set me apart.

'Gurney's the only one with a private room,' says Daphne.

'But what about the Head?'

'Even he has to share with Fairlie Brown. And there's only been a cease-fire in it since the Boss died.'

'I wish there were a Boss here today,' I say. 'But I'll go now and have a look at the Infant classrooms.'

The probationers put me right about the three estates of my

Infant Department. Marjorie is at present in Room Three with Primary Two B, Shirley is in Room Two with Primary Two A, and the Infants Mistress has hitherto been in Room One with Primaries One B and One A, since last year these two classes were too small to make two separate classes. And there is only one class-room available in any case, Marjorie says.

This morning, since I am in charge of the school (a fact both flattering and intimidating) I have to make a gesture of standing in the corridor and watching the classes filing in from the play-ground. In no time at all, all the doors are closed and there is silence. I think this is a pleasant change from Garlock St, where voices penetrated through doors – teachers' voices, prophesying war.

I look at the back playground and sigh with relief. No dingy tenement windows stare rudely down into it. A mellow grey stone wall surrounds it, and above, the heathery hills look down beyond it to the blue Clyde estuary with its loveliness. The fever, the fret and the fustiness of Garlock St are things fading rapidly away.

May
1950

As I make my way at last to my classroom, I think that although Fairlie Brown has gone, all is so quiet that I am lulled into feeling that no alarms or excursions can possibly invade this haven of rest that is Heatherbrae.

When I enter the classroom I am more amazed. It seems that either half of the class is absent or has been mislaid. Instead of the close-packed, forty-odd pupils I had in Garlock St, here I can count only twenty-five expectant infants spaced out in old-fashioned dual desks clamped to the floor, as in faraway times in the last school. At least Garlock St had new furniture.

I do not know whether to be gratified at the small number of children, many very well-dressed, or to be depressed by the antiquated background into which they are set. The room has pitch-pine panelling up to shoulder level, and above are glass partitions. This type of classroom design seems to have pervaded schools since Victoria sat on the throne.

The distinction which this room has, however, lies in the desks, which look as if they have been here since the Regency. Even in the days of my training in Glasgow I never saw such age-old desks as these. So old are they, indeed, that the clamps are set into nearly burrowed-out holes in the wavy wooden floor which can hardly hold the screws. At any minute one of these desks could disappear into whatever caverns lie beneath.

In one corner stands a gas-cooker which looks as if it had been made from war-time scrap or bits of a bombed tank. In order to reach my desk (high style) I have to circumvent this iron-clad hazard. I am sure I detect a whiff of gas, too.

At the back of the room, as if to compensate for the disintegrating furniture, are Gothic windows, noble enough to grace Cologne Cathedral. They are three in number and symmetrically arranged, one in the middle and two slightly smaller on either side of it. All they need to complete them are three saintly teachers in stained glass.

Curious, I move up to them, and, by standing on tiptoe, succeed in seeing the view from them. And this view exceeds in magnificence any of Miss Grott's holiday brochures. I can see the panorama of the Clyde estuary down to the Gareloch and up the river to the Rock of Dumbarton. The tide is low and the sandbanks are there. Immediately below on the shore are the ship-yards, birthplace of mighty ships, and mercifully with ships a-building in the stocks – stocks that were like skeletons in the 1930s.

I think, as I go back to the front, that I must see the next launching from here.

All the time I have been nosing around the room with its contradictions, there has been a hushed expectancy breathed by the twenty-five children. I can still hardly believe that I have the entire class. I bring out the keys that Marjorie had presented me with from a key-box in the staffroom, and which she says fit the locks in this room.

I begin by inserting a key in the desk. I discover that it is not even locked, and that when I try to lock it, the key refuses to perform such a menial chore. But inside I find a class register. It has

43

only twenty-seven names on it, so there are only two absentees. The right size of class at last!

The children have begun now to talk. They tell me that their jotters are in the cupboard under the blackboard. This blackboard is fixed to the wall, and there seems to have been a space below it which the miserly architect could not bear to ignore.

One key – a bent one – miraculously opens this cupboard. Inside, I find a treasure – an old brown hot-water pipe, which is so familiar to me that it is as if it had run underground from Garlock St and emerged here in Heatherbrae. I can now be assured of well-heated cupboards in the winter. Garlock St was built in the 1890s, Heatherbrae still further back, in the 1870s. I make a note to the effect that the next school I go to will be one built in modern times. Whether the architecture will be any more pleasing is not guaranteed. Rumours of schools full of synthetic walls and floors, wide open interiors, and surrounded by walls of glass, come percolating into staffrooms, but whether they will be more or less comfortable than those of the past is still to be discovered. At any rate, just now I am ready to risk it. And then there are promises of all sorts of amenities such as spacious dining-halls, gymnasia, playing-fields, assembly rooms, crafts rooms, medical offices and smooth hygienic flooring. I hardly think I shall live long enough for all this.

I look around me and try to imagine this fantasy taking place. Out of one of the other (unGothic) windows, I see the existing dining-hall – an unlovely prefabricated hut in the girls' playground.

I set to work to collect the milk and dinner money. Fine and easy here, with only twenty-five to be fed. Absolutely simple, the way I have always imagined it should be. But I wonder what I must do with it, now that it has been collected. I am still wondering, when the door opens and a boy comes in with a cash box. He offers it to me.

'Dinner money from Miss Greene,' he says and departs.

The door opens again before I can make any comment, and a girl appears with a similar box.

'Dinner money from Miss McGarvey and Miss Steele.' Soon

44

I have all the dinner money for the whole school. I must find out what the next step is in this school. The only one near enough is my probationer, Shirley.

'Oh,' she says. 'The Head – or Fairlie Brown – usually phones in the numbers to the Central Kitchen. At least, I think that's what they do. I've never done it myself, of course – '

'I take it the phone's in the Head's room.'

Phones were installed in schools during the War, not for educational purposes, but for War emergencies. And they have lingered on.

'What about the milk numbers?'

'Just give these to the janitor and the dinners to the Head. Sorry, of course, there's no Head.'

'No legs or arms either,' I say.

I make my way to the Head's room. Before I reach it, I hear a loud knocking. When I catch up with the source of this noise, it is to find a mighty woman in dungarees vigorously banging on the Head's door. She wheels round upon me belligerently.

'Where is he?' she shouts.

'Who?' I ask.

'Him.'

'Him?'

'Aye – him as tell't my Francis to get oot o' his road, when he went tae ask aboot his shorts.'

'Oh!' I say, with a vague feeling that I have heard something about shorts recently.

'He's in there. Just wait till I get my hauns on him!'

For answer I open the door and go in. The woman in dungarees, who is fighting her own private battle of the bulge, pushes in behind me.

'Whaur is he?' she says, looking round.

'Who?' I ask again.

'That man Brown.'

'Mr Brown is out of the school today – at a funeral, the funeral of the Headmaster.'

For a moment she seems deflated.

'When'll he be back?'

'Not today. Can I make a note of your complaint and pass it on?'

'That's no' the same. I'll come back tomorrow and hae it oot wi' him.'

'Maybe you'd better let me have the boy's name and tell me what happened.'

But it is some time and many circumlocutions later that I learn that she is Mrs Gillogaley and that she washes buses every morning down at the Service Depot. This is for the purpose, she says, of earning enough to buy her wee Francis and his six brothers pairs of shorts and sand-shoes for them new-fangled Gym things. It is a lot of nonsense, for there's nae Gym hall anyway. But she'll not be regarded as a parent who neglects her boys. They lose their sand-shoes every week, too. And if they lose any mair shorts they'll just have to go without them. She adds that she will take the skin off Francis's back if he loses another pair. But this time Francis says they were stolen, and this man wouldn't listen to a word he said when he reported it. And so on – and so on.

I am at a pitch of nervous tension listening to all this, and wondering simultaneously about the phoning that's still to be done about the dinners, as well as about the class, who must by this time be causing a breach of the peace to the disturbance of the lieges.

Mrs Gillogaley finishes her tirade with, 'I don't know who you are – never seen you before – but you can tell that man Brown that I'll be up tomorrow – after his funeral.'

I think it ought to be more correctly 'before his funeral'. But I am more than relieved at last to see the fully-filled dungarees present a broad beam to me on their journey to the door.

I rush to the phone. The Central Kitchen says that I nearly didn't get any dinners for the school today, as it's well over the time for the order, but they'll see what they can do. I am so distraught that I feel mince, turnip and potatoes with plum duff to follow will be the most acceptable of meals.

I dash back to ask the janitor about the milk, but he is nowhere to be found. I investigate a flight of steps descending into a dungeon just outside the back door, where I suspect the furnace room

46

lies. It is empty of both janitor and coal, it being the balmy summer-time.

I go to the classroom, where, surprisingly, the class sits semi-silent, watching two boys delivering a crate of milk bottles. From the class I learn that milk comes every day like this, and no effort required on my part. I am wondering why I have been chosen to take charge, I who depend on probationers and poppets for my potential.

I open the pipe-ridden cupboard to look for the jotters the class promised I should find there. These turn out to be a collection resembling three-thousand-year-old papyri just excavated from an Egyptian tomb. They almost crumble in the light of day. My instinct is to dump them in the waste basket, but another instinct, professionally indoctrinated, steps in and warns me to retain the jotters in case of Aitch-Em-Ayes – Inspectors who might descend on us at any time. Reason says that no Inspectors are likely to come so near to the summer holidays. But I return the jotters, gingerly, to the cupboard. I intend that, should the worst come to the worst, I shall disclaim them.

I find a pile of slates, the antiques mentioned earlier in the staffroom, and look at them in wonder. It is years since I saw slates. There is also beside them a box of slate pencils designed to squeak on the slates.

I take a sudden decision. I shall use the slates but in conjunction with handfuls of chubby coloured chalks which I have brought from Garlock St. The slates make a terrific clatter and the chalks a terrific dust. But Primary One AB fall upon them with whoops of delight. All we need to complete the picture of pavement artists are caps for alms.

Grateful for the creative silence, I insinuate myself among the desks to find out who is who in the class. I think too of how I shall plan an educational revolution in Heatherbrae which apparently has been snoring for years in the sleep of stagnation.

I am dreaming this dream when there is a knock on the door. I find a middle-aged woman standing outside.

'I've come to take Agnes to the Clinic,' she says.

'Agnes who?' I ask.

'McKim. She's to get a dip injection. And she gets cod-liver oil and orange juice as well.'

I call out Agnes, but although she is to get all these lovely things, there is no response.

'Where is Agnes McKim?' I call again.

I go to investigate. Agnes is there, but huddled out of sight below the desk. She sets up a mighty howl when I reach down to prise her out.

'Better come in and fetch her yourself,' I say. 'She'll maybe come out for her mother.'

'Oh, I'm no' her mother. Her mother's in the hospital wi' another wean. I'm her Granny.'

The Granny produces a piece of chocolate, but it is some time before this is a strong enough lure. Finally, Granny lifts her bodily and bears her off, whimpering.

The earlier peacefulness of the class is now shattered.

'When do we get our juice, please, miss?'

'You'll hear about that soon, I hope,' I say, stalling.

'I get cod-liver oil!' shouts another voice.

'I hate cod-liver oil! I like juice.'

The tongues are no longer tied, and I am proved no disciplinarian today. The chattering goes on, gaining decibels. I must remember, too, that these are no mere beginners. They are veterans of six months' standing who know more about this school than I.

There is yet another knock on the door. The woman outside says, 'I've come to take William for his injection.'

'William who?'

'Bradley. I was hoping, miss, that William would get somebody next term who understands him. The last teacher never understood William. He's full of nerves.'

I call out, 'William Bradley. Here's your mother.'

'Oh, no. I'm not his mother. His mother's out working. I'm his Auntie.'

The misunderstood William comes at once and hides his face in his Auntie's skirt. I almost shove them out. If I have any more of this, I'll be full of nerves and need an injection.

48

I shut the door with finality, and wish I had a bolt for it. But I am no sooner on my rounds of the desks again than there is another knock. I descend on it with the expression of a wolf on the fold just as it is pushed open and another woman this time actually comes into the room unasked!

Then I notice she has a sheaf of papers in her hand. Ominous! I say: 'Is it for another injection? And who is it this time?'

'His Majesty's Inspector. I'm Miss Graham. I'm told you are in charge of the school today. Sorry to come upon you like this, but we did inform the Headmaster.'

'He died!' I say, then think this is tactless. 'Mr Brown is away at the funeral. This is my first day here as Infants Mistress.'

'You poor dear!' she says sympathetically. 'I think, if it suits you all right, we'll repair to the Head's room, and see you after the interval.'

I see the janitor on his way to ring the bell.

'Yes,' goes on Miss Graham (the first woman Inspector I have ever seen), 'there are three of us – Mr McKechnie and Dr Gregor, the Chief Inspector, as well as myself. We'll divide the classes between us.'

I really wish they would.

Vera Brown has seen the Inspectors coming into the school and has duly warned the others. She takes from the staffroom cupboard a number of cups (with saucers) which she says are kept purely for Inspectors. From her tone it might seem as if these are the ones with the henbane in them.

Finally, cups of quite innocent tea and some biscuits (ostentatiously gifted by Mrs Whyte) are borne along to the Head's room. In this school, however, it seems that the Staff take Inspectors fairly lightly, and any fears are affectations in keeping with the changing attitude of the times, or maybe because of the rarefied atmosphere peculiar to Heatherbrae.

'Dr Gregor gets a name for being a bit of a wag,' says Rita McGarvey. 'He just loves to take the class for a lesson, and forgets to do any other inspecting, once he gets going.'

'I could cheerfully hand them over to him for the rest of the forenoon,' I say, 'so that I could find out more about where things are in this school.'

'It's really quite simple,' says Rita. 'You'll have learned it by tomorrow.'

'It's a relief from Garlock St,' I say. 'It was a factory.'

'This is a home industry,' says Vera Brown. 'And, to encourage it, you'll get a lot of money to spend.'

'Me? How's that?'

'Anybody foolhardy enough to be an Infants Mistress is given a sum of money to spend on the Department, so I'm told.'

'I've never been told,' I say. 'Nobody ever tells me anything.'

'Be sure you ask Fairlie Brown about it,' she warns. 'Headmasters, too, are sometimes reluctant to divulge it. Which makes me wonder who we'll get for a Head.'

Who-we'll-get provides the topic for the rest of the interval. I could do with whoever-we'll-get right now, to take charge of the three Fates sitting in his room.

The interval is a full quarter of an hour in Heatherbrae, another improvement on Garlock St, where every necessity had to be crowded into ten minutes. In Heatherbrae there is time to finish a cigarette – 'and no big ends left,' says Rita, stubbing out a half-inch.

'Does the Head – did the Head – not object to smoking?' I ask.

'He smoked a foul black pipe himself,' she says. 'And had a foul black temper to match. God rest his soul!'

I am Dr Gregor's first victim. He comes into my room like a half-gale blowing up the Firth of Clyde. His handshake resembles the Boot and his voice the foghorn at the Cloch Lighthouse.

'So you're in charge of the whole school, eh?'

'For today,' I say.

'Tomorrow will be easier, you'll see.'

I think that if he and his henchmen had not arrived, it would have been easier today. But I do him a wrong, for it is Fairlie Brown who is to blame for not passing on the information before escaping to the cemetery.

'I don't know where all the material is,' I say.

'The last time I inspected there was little or no material. You must change all that. Order lots of material – things to handle, things to examine, things to make.'

'I brought up my own collection from Garlock St – to be going on with.'

'Oh, so you're from Garlock St. Grim – grim – needs painting inside. Needs new toilets. That's another thing I must discuss with you – toilets.'

I could have thought of more stimulating subjects, and one less redolent of Garlock St.

'Seeing you have nothing on hand as yet, I'll just talk to the class. This is not really a formal inspection. Just a general view, and some recommendations.'

He moves to a central position half-way between the door and the windows. I move awkwardly round the cooker to my desk.

'You must get rid of that cooker,' he says. He faces the class.

'Now, children – '

He waits patiently until every eye is upon him. I have to admit he has a personal magnetism and a relaxed attitude which I suppose is the New Look for HMIs. But I fervently hope that whatever report may be made will be favourable since I am responsible for the school today.

He speaks to the class in a boy-to-boy tone.

'I'm not going to listen to you reading today, nor ask you to count or write. I am sure you know quite a lot about counting already, anyway – '

This encouragement causes a hand to shoot up at the back, and a voice calls out,

'I know what a hundred times one is.'

'That's very good. What's your name?'

'Bobby Farquharson.'

'Do you keep your eyes open, Bobby?'

'Ye-es,' says Bobby, and adds, ' 'Cept in bed.'

'What I meant was, do you watch what goes on around you – for instance, what people work at in this town?'

Another hand starts waving at the side.

'My Daddy's an ice-cream man. He's got a van.'

'That's fine. But what goes on down at the river out there? Surely some of your fathers work in the ship-yards.'

More hands start waving about.

'Ah – a lot, eh! Now, then, tell me something important that happened yesterday down at one of the ship-yards . . .'

Dr Gregor finally selects one hand. 'A man got hurted. He fell off a cran.'

'Really? I didn't know that. What I really meant was that a big ship was built, and now you tell me what happened to it yesterday.'

Only one hand is raised.

'A liner was launched,' says the owner of the hand.

'Ah – now – that's what I was after. And do you know its name?'

'Oh, yes. The *McTaratan Tower*.'

'Very good. What's your name?'

'Augustus Ponsonby, 52 Rosetree Avenue.'

'Did you go to see the launch, Augustus?'

'Oh, yes. My Daddy's a Director.'

'Really? Did anybody else see the launch?'

Several hands go up. The voices begin:

'My Daddy's a hauder-on.'

'Mine's a caulker.'

'Fine,' says Dr Gregor. 'While everybody stands watching for the launch to begin, something happens. What's that?'

The voices come again –

'Everybody shouts!'

'Anything else?'

'The ship goes into the water.'

'Ah, yes – but you haven't told me what happens before that.' Silence. Even from Augustus.

'The ship gets christened – gets its name, that fine name Augustus mentioned. Now, who christens it?'

'The Minister!'

'No. Not the Minister this time.'

'A lady!' This from Augustus.

52

'That's right. Who can tell me what she christens it with?'

Silence.

'You are christened with water. But the ship – what about it?'

The class seems to have exhausted its stock of information.

'It's with a bottle of something,' goes on the helpful Dr Gregor.

'Coca-Cola!'

'Lemonade!'

'No. I'm afraid I'll have to tell you after all. The lady bashes a bottle against the ship's side and calls out its name.'

'I've seen that!'

'So've I.'

'Of course you have!' Relief in his tone. He is determined to pursue the lesson to the bitter end.

'The bottle has not got Coca-Cola in it, nor lemonade either. It has champagne in it. Now, what's champagne?'

The silence this time is profound. The puzzlement purls a few brows, and eyes are rolled up to the ceiling. I am sure champagne is well outwith their slight experience. If it had been Guinness now – or Pale Ale –

'Ah, Augustus!' says Dr Gregor. 'What's champagne then?'

'I think,' says Augustus rather doubtfully, 'I think it's a kind of grown-ups' juice.'

Suddenly Dr Gregor looks at his watch. 'Dear me! Is it that time already? I don't know when to stop once I'm in front of a class. I enjoyed that. Very responsive bunch, I must say. Grown-ups' juice, eh? Very stimulating. Perhaps we could pay a visit now to your cloakrooms and see what's to be done about the wash-basins.'

As we reach the cloakroom, Dr Gregor says, 'Where do you keep the toilet roll?'

'Toilet roll?'

'Oh, yes. Surely you have a supply by this time. All schools should have been supplied by this time.'

'Well,' I say, 'when Mr Brown comes back, I'll ask –'

'I'll make a note that they are not in evidence here yet. A

toilet roll must be put in a suitable place. Now, let's see, where could you put it here?'

I am as puzzled as he is.

'Ah!' he says, as with inspiration, 'the very place!' And he points out a ledge above the wash-basin. 'That would do nicely.'

I have an uneasy feeling that the bell has been on that ledge, but I do not like to discourage him.

'Oh, yes,' I say. 'But we'll have to – eh – instruct the children – infants will surely have to be given some kind of – instruction – shown how to – take their – eh – ration, as it were – I suppose it will apply to the whole school – '

'Of course – of course,' says he, 'the whole school will have to use toilet rolls. Right from the bottom up, you know.'

'Right from the bottom up!' says Vera Brown today as I enter the staffroom. 'I expect they've been using that wisecrack in every school on their rounds.'

Rita and Rena come in at that moment, looking as if they cannot suppress some news.

'What's that I hear?' says Rita. 'Bottoms up?'

'We've just been to Mother McCrae's wee shop at the foot of the brae,' says Rena. 'We went in to buy cigarettes.'

'And who do you think came in while we were there?' says Rita.

'Dr Gregor?' says Daphne. 'He smokes. I heard the Inspectors are still in the district. Going to Garlock St today.'

'It wasn't Dr Gregor,' says Rena. 'It was Tom McCrone and his wee brother.'

'And what of it?' says Vera.

'They were carrying a toilet roll apiece,' says Rita.

'Dr Gregor's recommendation has been taken to heart then,' I say.

'Since the McCrone family moved into their council house,' says Vera, 'there's no holding them back. Addie McCrone told me yesterday they were inviting some friends to tea.'

'Oh, yes,' says Rena. 'They invited the friends.'

'And,' goes on Rita, 'when we were in the shop, Tommy and

his brother came in and laid the two toilet rolls on the counter.'
Rita stops and giggles. 'You tell the rest, Rena.'

'Tommy said to Mother McCrae, "Me mammy says will ye take back them toilet rolls and swap them for six Woodbines. The visitors didny turn up." '

May
1950

Having survived my first day as Infants Mistress of Heather-brae, I feel the worst is surely over, and temporarily tattered or not, I shall now be free to pursue my plans for being all a modern Infants Mistress should be.

I am rather flattered to find that I am referred to as the 'Head-mistress' by a number of the parents, and this title is not attri-butable to my deputizing for the Head on the first day. It really originated in days gone by when the Infants Mistress was recog-nized for her true worth as a power in the land. She was ack-nowledged then as the one upon whose success as a foundation stone all the future careers of the school population were raised. I sigh a little for this lost status, only a fraction of an inch below that of the Headmaster, and which of late has become universally shrunk from Vice-Admiral to Petty Officer.

I am determined to work for the reinstatement of the past

image of the Headmistress. I make up my mind, not only to establish new ways of teaching, but to introduce a New Look in Infants Mistresses – she who will fall foul of neither child, parent nor Staff, who will be full of consideration for all, who will be the exponent of tact and wisdom. Even the janitor, no matter how cross-grained, will be treated like the rest. In this school, I privately think, it is just possible that Mr Gurney has been misunderstood, poor man.

Since my first harrowing day, I have had to repeat the attractions of the chalk-and-slate activity. Today I improve on this by issuing large sheets of brown and grey drawing paper which measure twelve inches by ten. Away with the seven by seven of those miserable drawing books. I have these large sheets because I encountered Fairlie Brown's boys bearing them to the bin. He is a devotee of the seven by seven Art School of Japanese miniatures. Certainly the twelve by ten – as well as some twelve by fifteen which are even better – which he was throwing out, were not in their pristine perfection, but they warranted a better fate than the bin. Sheer waste. It has only occurred to me now that maybe it was not Fairlie himself who did the cupboard clearing, but the boys, who in any case run his class for themselves and do all the chores.

The amount of dust from the big sheets, scrubbed on by crayons held in twenty-seven fists, is creating a miasma. I open the classroom door to allow the cloud to rush out, and immediately a large Labrador dog rushes in. It runs among the desks, and the class is thrown into confusion, but enjoys every minute of it. Sheets of paper are blown onto the floor by the whirlwind tour. The dog dashes finally for the open door. I pursue it to make sure its ejection into the street will be final.

It makes along the corridor for the front door of the school, someone in the first instance having been guilty of leaving that door open. I spend a precious moment shutting the classroom door and the door leading to the playground as if there were a fire emergency.

When I reach the front of the school again, it is standing peacefully at the steps leading down to the main gate. With soft words and false promises I entice it as far as the gate. If I can get it to move outside, I shall swing the big school gates together and exclude it for all time. It stands firm.

I feel it would be futile to push it. Have you ever tried pushing a dog which maybe weighs a hundred and twenty pounds? I once did in the last school, and it immediately turned into a mule. So I go out into the street and talk to it from there. I feel thankful that there are only the windows of villas across the street and not a whole row of tenement grandstands. The Provost lives directly across the street and a handsome ornamental lamp-post with the Burgh coat-of-arms on it stands imposingly outside his gate.

The situation is saved by a Scots terrier approaching this august lamp-post. The Labrador dashes over and the Scots terrier makes off. As if in disgust, the Labrador insults the post. But by this time I have swung the gates together with an almighty clang. I mount the steps to go back into the school and the dog barks furiously through the gates.

'Off home!' I shout from the safety of the steps. 'Off! And don't come back!' Which having said, I turn round and cannon into the enraged face of the janitor emerging from the front door. He rushes past me, runs down the steps and flings open the gates again. The big Labrador bounds up on him and licks his face. He takes it by the collar and guides it back up the steps.

'You may be the Headmistress,' he shouts, 'but ye'll no' pit oot my Caesar like that!'

'Your – Caesar?'

'Aye – and if it wasna for my Caesar ye widna hae a janitor. I've to be in this school at five every morning tae pit on the furnace, and it's Caesar that guards me all the way up right frae the toon. They should provide a hoose at the school, so they should.'

'But you don't put on the furnace in summer-time,' I say defensively.

'If you think I'm getting rid o' Caesar just for the summer, ye're wrong. Never was a dog like Caesar!'

'Are you allowed to have a dog in the school all day?' I say (recalling the dog-in-the-toilet tale). 'Does Mr Brown know?'

'Him!' (A great many people seem to prefer Him as a name for Fairlie.) 'Who cares for him? He's aye greetin' aboot the break-ins. He's just got tae pit up wi' Caesar.' And he stumps up the steps with a righteous expression.

It is so important, in every school you go to, to make a friend of the janitor.

But I fear that there are other problem personalities besides Old Gurney. One is Fairlie Brown himself. And it is now obvious why Vera Brown is not flattered at being taken for his wife.

The noise emanating from Fairlie's classroom is something to make history. It is not one continuous noise, like a city railway station or a football match, but it comes in great nerve-shattering bursts. Until I heard it for myself, I was prepared to discount Ailie Chapman's embittered protests, Ailie teaching – or trying to teach – next door to him.

'And to think,' she says, 'that he earns more than I do, and for less years of teaching. And does damn all.'

This is strong brew for Ailie, who is over sixty and has been a Sunday School teacher for much of her life.

'It's high time we all had equal pay,' says Rena Steele. 'Teachers will not always be so plentiful. Wait until the post-war Bulge gets bigger.'

'He gets responsibility payment as well,' goes on Ailie. 'Like you,' she adds, a thought unfairly in the context.

'A princely £35,' I say.

'You seem to earn yours.'

I bow in acknowledgement. 'I try,' I say. 'But I've never been in his classroom. How do we know that he doesn't earn it?'

I am now on the responsibility echelon myself, so I feel we ought to hold together.

'Take a walk along the corridor any day,' says Rena. 'If it's quiet, you'll know he's not in his classroom. But when he is – '

The beginners are at school only in the mornings for the first months of their school life, so I am able to catch up on the multi-farious items needing attention. This afternoon I am peacefully turning out a large cupboard in the staffroom to see if I can create more space for new materials. I am near the back window which is open, when I hear the phone ringing in the Head's room.

It goes on and on. I go to investigate and enter the Head's room by the door from the annexe. I pick it up and it is someone from the Education Offices asking for Mr Brown. I go out by the other door which leads to the corridor where his classroom is.

Before I reach it I hear a shindy in progress. As I draw near there is an almighty crash. It sounds as if one of the eight-foot-high solid wooden blackboards with which this school is provided has overturned, destroying everything in its path. I am in doubt whether to run for the janitor's first-aid box or brave the battle-field firmly. I throw open the classroom door and enter, my hand on my scabbard.

Then I just stand and stare.

Boys are hopping from the top of one desk to the next all over the room. They gleefully push one another to the ground with whoops of joy. I look for the prone blackboard, but this hefty eight-footer stands firmly in position, the only quiet thing in the room. The class apparently disdain any of the injunctions to work written upon it.

I look for Fairlie Brown himself. I have decided he is out, then remember what Rena said. Suddenly a face rises up from the back desks and Fairlie extricates himself from a dozen mixed boys and girls.

'Just showing them a little problem,' he shouts above the din. 'But it's a bit complicated, you know. Were you wanting any-thing?'

'I don't, but the Education Office does. Your phone's been ringing – '

'Never hear it in this room,' he says. 'Wish we had another Headmaster. Save me always answering it.'

He goes out to do this back-breaking chore. A few books are thrown about as I make my retreat. A few boys are trying a hand-stand on top of the long-suffering desks. Another is creeping underneath and one of the girls is pulling a long nauseating tendril of chewing-gum out of her vacuous mouth. I am far from the mêlée by the time Fairlie is on his way back. He comes hurry-ing after me, flapping a paper in his hand.

'I clean forgot to give you this,' he says. 'Came in ten days ago. With all these complications of the Boss dying it slipped my memory.'

He thrusts the paper into my hand and rushes back to his Chaos and Old Night.

I meet Ailie Chapman emerging from her classroom with the look of an Amazon on her face and a pointer clutched in her hand like a Lochaber axe.

'I'm not putting up with it another minute,' she says. 'It's been going on since lunch-time.'

'I know what you mean now,' I say. 'But whom do you complain to? Don't go in there just now. It's full of wild Highlanders. By the way, what was that fearful crash a while ago?'

'It's the one mystery I've never solved,' she says. 'But it happens from time to time. I think he must hit the desk with his strap.'

'Shouldn't he hit the kids with it?'

'I think he's too scared,' she says. 'But I'm going in this time, First Assistant or not.'

'Why didn't the last Head do something about it?'

'Fairlie was his son-in-law,' and still clutching the pointer, she opens his door.

I do not wait on the outcome, for I am staring at the letter. It asks the Head to inform the new Infants Mistress that she will now be able to make a requisition for stock for her department up to the value of £100. The last paragraph says that the order must be presented at the end of the week.

I sit down to recover from the shock of this. As the blood returns to my bemused brain, I look at the date on the letter. It appears that I am at least seven days overdue in taking advantage of this amazing offer. Was that the subject of the phone call to Fairlie Brown?

I rush along to ask him in order to square myself with the Administration. I find his class dismissed although the bell has not yet been rung. I knock on the Head's door, and he appears with his hat on.

'Look here,' I say, deciding to follow up Ailie Chapman's effort at intimidation, although I see no scars obvious on his person. 'This is news to me.' I wave the letter in my hand.

'I've a meeting in Glasgow,' he says, pushing past me, 'an important meeting about school discipline. I'm the County delegate.'

He is more than half-way to the door, but I pursue.

'You'll find plenty of catalogues in the Head's cupboard,' he shouts back. 'Make up the requisition from them.'

'But it's overdue!' I scream. 'You'd better phone tomorrow and tell them why it's late – '

My words have lost their force, for by this time he is down the steps and on his way to delegate discipline.

A hundred pounds! A whole hundred pounds to spend! If I had been given it as a bonus to my salary I could not have been more astonished. I am sure that the list of items I now begin to envisage could never possibly amount to such a fantastic sum. What do I do with all the money which is sure to be left over? Did he say catalogues? Let me get my hands on them and begin that orgy of ordering.

I plunge into the Head's cupboard in a frenzy of discovery. If a real Head were here, I should never have been able to have such a rummage. Ha! six sonsy volumes in handsome bindings, and all this year's issue.

Never before have I been able to handle even one catalogue. In my last school only the Head teacher had access to these holy books. The Infants Mistress herself had to submit her requests to him, whereupon he would look up the catalogue to see how much it was going to cost the rate-payers. He would then blue-pencil all her hopes, almost as if it was to come out of his own salary. The result, of course, was poverty, the poverty I found in the cupboards of Heatherbrae when I came. The catalogues were then returned to the Head's cupboard, or in some instances, to his safe, as if they were rare volumes of classical pornography.

I pick up the catalogues reverently and turn a few tentative pages. I am amazed to see so many new aids to learning offered so prodigally. I take home the catalogues to gloat upon them in private. My cherished plans for advancement in this Infant Department shall soon be realized, once all the equipment is here.

I shall not be mean either, and keep them to myself. My two assistants will be allowed to inspect them and make suggestions, of which they have been so shamefully starved in the past. I am fast becoming a really democratic boss on this munificent £100.

I have now made out a list culled from the coloured catalogues, and have received a bonus of acclaim from Shirley and Marjorie. I ask them to pick out anything they think will fit in with all the new ideas they learned at College but have never been able to use for lack of equipment.

I write out two sheets of foolscap with my requests upon them – 'things to make, things to examine, things to handle' – as instructed by Dr Gregor.

And the books! No more Victorian reach-me-downs or nursery-rhyme people dressed in Edwardian clothes. What is more, no more tattered readers with covers hanging by a thread. Every book will be new, gay and bright. None will be boring. We shall have a library full of pretty princesses, brilliant birds, fairy lands, as well as real adventure.

All the books will be different. No more hand-outs of the same volume for all to read at the same place at the same time at the same rate. I come upon the very thing, newly-published, full of variety. I eagerly enter the titles on my list. Even the titles glow with colour. They are arranged in sets of each colour (twelve different books in each set.) Just the thing. So I put down:

'One dozen Red Stories.' I follow this by 'One dozen Yellow Stories'. Then I finally add 'One dozen Blue Stories'.

Today I add the lists of prices up and find they come to £200!

Shirley Greene hands her list in during the morning and it has come to £50.

Marjorie Black follows hot-foot with a list totalling £75.

Clearly, being generous and democratic is not feasible. Shame-facedly I recant, and like the old Head teachers in the old contemptible schools, I blue-pencil extravagantly, as extravagantly as I had ordered – my own as well as theirs.

I am puzzled by Shirley's list. 'Look here,' I say to her. 'What's this? Six canes – six leather straps – six leather sets for strait-lacing – three hammers, three chisels. Is it murder you contemplate or only a beginner's course in burglary?'

'You asked us for our order.'

'I know – but what are these for?'

'Oh, the canes are for jumping over at Gym – '

'But the straps?'

'Some children can't fix their belts or lace their shoes. These are for practising on.'

'And the hammers and chisels?'

'You want us to begin crafts. I think they should learn to use tools.'

'You omitted the jemmies,' I say, 'and I'm afraid you'll maybe get only the canes this year. We're well over the amount offered.'

This is a bitter anti-climax for me, an ignominious climbing down. I am learning fast that being on the upper rungs of the ladder means that you have further to fall.

I take home the orders and reduce them by various mathematical stratagems to £100. It looks a meagre enough sheet of foolscap when I take it along to Fairlie Brown. I feel a sympathy with the dunces of old who wore the foolscap on their heads.

'Don't forget to send this,' I say, laying it on his desk.

'You'll never get all that,' he says, lifting up a blue pencil from the desk.

'No censoring!' I say, in such a sharp tone that he hastily lays down the pencil.

'And it should have been sent off a week ago, and you know that. I may not even get it in time now. Thank goodness that's the last bit of ordering for this session.'

'Oh no, it's not,' says he, and places another sheet before me. 'You've still to order the sewing material for the whole school.'

'But shouldn't that have been done by the last Infants Mistress before she moved out?'

'She didn't do it, so it's your responsibility. You're qualified to teach sewing, I believe.'

I now see the folly of having extra qualifications. And I don't get a penny of responsibility payment for that one. Some day there will be a rebellion.

I spend my only free time today touring the school to find out how many there will be for sewing. This, of course, means all the girls. The boys are supposed to be taught Arts and Crafts, and, this being interpreted, generally means arithmetic. Fairlie Brown is not qualified to teach Arts and Crafts, so his contingent is unloaded upon Ailie Chapman, who is boiling up to assassination point.

I find there are a hundred and fifty girls for sewing. I divide them up into lots of twenty-six per class, a reasonable number, I think, and nobody can object to that. No sweated labour here. But after I have allotted the twenty-six to all the available teachers, I have forty-six left over. I can either take these myself like a martyr, or suffer yet another ignominy and be forced to confess that I am not the expert organizer I believed myself to be. So I take on the forty-six. It will not happen till next session, of course. And I comfort myself with the thought that I shall have a long summer holiday to charge up for the fray.

In the staffroom they all look at me as they would a martyr about to be consumed.

'Are you really going to take on forty-six?'

'I have handled more,' I say airily.

'Will we be making anything new?' This from Ailie Chapman, who on principle dislikes anything new.

'Possibly,' I say. 'Kettle holders and Dutch aprons are not very exciting. What use are Dutch aprons, anyway? Imagine Mrs Gillogaley wearing a Dutch apron!'

'My girls will tackle anything,' says Daphne Whyte. 'With my long married experience, that's to be expected, of course.'

I do not get the correct thought connection here, surely. It seems to me Daphne overdoes the married life – or death, for Daphne has had a double widowhood. And is looking for another, Vera says, ambiguously.

I sit up late with last year's copies of the sewing requisition, and I am depressed by the dreariness of the cloth we are offered. It seems exactly the same as it has been for the last twenty years, even more utility than 'Utility'. Its usefulness is in question too, as I cannot see it yielding to scissors. I expect some eyebrows will be raised when I produce nothing new as far as the cloth goes. I feel they are all expecting a new era of muslin, damask and satin.

I am not happy either about the progress my class is making. The environment overwhelms me more than it does the children. The old iron sink and the army barracks cooker depress me.

The 'glass' blackboard refuses to be written on, and the chalk skates when I try to draw any figures on it. Shirley and Marjorie keep complaining about the galleries in their classrooms and the gloom thrown by 40-watt lamps which ought to be 100-watt lamps. Shirley's blackboard is pockmarked all over so that when she writes anything on it, the words are all interspersed with strange shapes that look like inscriptions in cuneiform.

The cloakroom has chipped wash-basins and the toilet roll has been deposed from the ledge selected by Dr Gregor. Mr Gurney was insulted that the dignified brass bell, in which he has the most inordinate pride, should be deposed for a thing like a toilet roll. Totally unnecessary, anyway, he declares.

I look hopelessly at the cloakroom. There is a cleaner's mop in one corner and below the wash-basins several pails and feather dusters. I marvel at the feather dusters which are still being faithfully used to remove dust from high up and disperse it to low down. I wonder if feather dusters are used in the Education Offices, or if up there they have heard of vacuum cleaners.

I hesitate to beard Mr Gurney in his den, not because of Caesar, but because I now see myself in a cold war with the male section of the school, the First Assistant and the janitor.

I vacillate between beginning abrasive tactics straight away tomorrow or waiting a little longer in the hope that some man of determinative character will soon be appointed as Head. I know the odds are a hundred to one against a Headmaster being appointed for such virtues as vision, versatility – or virility.

This is tomorrow, and the tough tactics which I have spent most of last night mentally rehearsing are temporarily suspended.

'I hear that a new Head has been appointed,' says Vera Brown in her quick, coiled-spring manner. She manages to jab in this news a fraction of a second before Daphne Whyte comes in, obviously ready to spring something upon us.

'I hear a new Head has been appointed,' she says breathlessly, the strands of her lank red hair quivering with excitement.

'So I have just been saying,' says Vera.

'Tell us more,' says Rena. 'Who is it? Anybody we know?'

'Far from it,' says Daphne quickly before Vera can get the lead again.

'Who?' says Rita.

'Somebody from the Highlands,' says Vera.

'Goodbye to new methods!' says Shirley.

'I'll be the one to decide that,' I say, putting some of the tough tactics into practice.

'Sorry,' says Shirley. 'Didn't mean our department.'

'What's his name?' I ask.

'Don't know yet,' admits Vera reluctantly. 'Do you know, Daphne?' But Daphne has to admit failure.

'Is he young or old?' asks Ailie, who believes crabbed age and youth cannot live together.

But nobody can answer this question either.

'I think he's unlikely to be a young man,' says Rita. 'He'll be sixty if he's a day, and working up to the last three years for his pension. It happens with monotonous regularity.'

'Who told you a Head had been appointed?' says Daphne to Vera.

'A friend of mine in St Swithin's.'

'Really? How on earth does a Greeninch school get to know these things before we do up here?'

'Their newly-appointed Maths teacher was up at an interview on the same day,' says Vera.

June
1950

I have made up my mind to tackle Fairlie Brown about the environment without delay. I am given impetus by the fear that a man of sixty emanating from the Highlands might be likely to think that an old iron sink, a cooker and dual desks are highly modern and desirable amenities compared to anything he has in his broch in Benbecula.

After I have demanded the removal of the sink and the cooker, the dual desks and the galleries, and am panting with the heat of my zeal and determination, Fairlie says:

'It shall be done.'

'Eh?'

'That's right. Your cooker's to go – and the sink and the galleries as well.'

'All of them?' I ask suspiciously.

'Some this year and some next year.'

'What about the cloakrooms?'

'What's wrong with them?'

I might have known that somebody like Fairlie would not see anything wrong with cloakrooms full of pails and dusters.

'They're full of cleaners' implements.'

'Take a look in Gurney's room and see if you can find a place for them there,' he says.

'How does it come about that all these things are really going to be done at last?'

'Dr Gregor's report.'

'He's the first Inspector then whose report has ever been taken seriously in my experience,' I say.

'The Master of Works was in yesterday taking a look.'

I feel quite benevolent towards Fairlie Brown for once. A Master of Works sounds impressive enough, a man of action, who might even do more than merely look.

'I believe,' I say, 'that the new Head has been appointed.'

'He'll be here next week.'

'Really? So near the end of the term?'

'Just like yourself.'

'Of course – but I didn't cut it as fine as that.' Although, I add to myself, fine enough.

'What's his name?'

'Fergus Ogg, from the Isle of Skye.'

'Old or young?'

'Middling – I think.'

'Married?'

'Not so far as I know. He's a graduate of Aberdeen University, MA and BSc.'

'Is teaching an art or a science?'

'What was that?'

'Our new Head has versatility.'

'Oh – eh – oh, yes. By the way, you'd better ask the janitor to get out that flag again.'

But I bypass the janitor's room and release my M I file on the Staff. Immediate reaction from Daphne.

'Isn't that a coincidence!' she says. 'I expect to be going to Skye for my holidays next year. I wonder if he's a McLeod.'

'An Ogg,' I say.

'A what?'

'An Ogg,' I say. 'Fergus Ogg.'

'Ogg,' says Ailie, 'as far as I know, means a younger son.'

'Is he young?'

'Fairlie says middling – he thinks. I expect,' I go on, 'that he'll be wearing a kilt and have a *sgian dhubh* in his thick hand-knitted stockings.'

'You're making all that up,' says Shirley.

'Don't listen to her,' says Rita. 'She's only pulling our legs.'

'If his stockings are hand-made,' says Daphne, 'he must be married.'

'I expect he plays the bagpipes too,' I say, 'and will want to encourage lessons on them in the school.'

'He'll never come to school in a kilt,' says Ailie seriously. 'It wouldn't be correct.'

'And why not?' says Vera.

'Whoever heard of a Headmaster in a kilt?'

'Schools would be brighter if they did,' says Vera.

I am tempted to continue the imaginary picture, but seeing the eager interest engendered in Daphne, I tell her that Fairlie Brown is of the opinion that Fergus Ogg is a bachelor.

She hurries away on the first tinkle of the bell, going, she says, to the hairdresser.

'Getting ready to ogle Ogg, isn't she?' says Vera. 'I'd better look out my best dress for the big day.'

'What about the flag?' asks Ailie. I wince at the reminder.

'It wasn't very robust when it was put up at the funeral. It nearly tore across when Gurney hoisted it. I don't think it will stand an inauguration.'

I don't think I shall stand an inauguration either.

'When was the flag made?' I ask.

'In 1895,' says Ailie. 'I was just a child then, and in the school for the first time. It was presented by a ship-builder who began here as a boy. He rose to the top when he grew up.'

'I hope his flag will, too – next week,' says Vera on her way out.

I decide to ignore the command of Fairlie Brown about seeing the janitor, and make up my mind to steal away unseen. But I am hailed by Gurney, who emerges from his cubicle enveloped in a vast sea of calico. As he shouts after me, I turn and see his hand suddenly burst through the shrouds. The hole widens and his face appears.

'Hey!' he shouts. 'Get this flag off me!'

I lay down my shopping bag and I am committed to detaching Gurney from the rotting folds of the school flag. It is an immense piece of decomposing cotton. As he finally steps out of it as from an antique crinoline, it subsides in the corridor like a parachute.

I call out – 'Don't tramp on it!'

'I was coming to find you,' he says. 'Mr First Assistant Brown says to have the flag up on Monday for that there new Head-master.'

'That's right,' I say gleefully. 'You'll have all the week-end to mend it.'

'It's you will have to do that,' he says.

'Me?'

'Aye. That there First Assistant says to hand it to you to get them holes mended. You're the sewing teacher, he says.'

The Staff are aghast today at the huge pile of frail cotton I had to leave last night on the staffroom table for lack of a better place to store it. Daphne Whyte and Ailie Chapman are gingerly lifting the folds that look as if they have just been removed from a three-thousand-year-old Egyptian mummy.

'That can never go up on the flagpole,' says Ailie. 'It had its last airing at the Head's death.'

'You can't see what the device is meant to be,' says Vera. 'Looks like a lot of nuts to me.'

'The whole thing's nuts,' says Shirley distastefully, lifting a corner and letting it drop again. 'Dump it.'

'Nobody could possibly mend that,' says Marjorie. 'Better put it in the bin.'

'Who'll put it there?' I say, 'and what bin?'

'That's all you young ones ever want,' says Ailie, 'just to get rid of anything that's old.'

At that moment Daphne comes in and removes her hat to reveal a perm. Although it makes her look like an egg-wet eaglet, the disappearance of the lank hair is a startling transformation, not necessarily for the better.

'What's that?' she says, the perm temporarily taking second place in her attention.

'The school flag,' says Rena, 'or what in days of yore was the school flag. Nobody could ever do anything with it now.'

'Yet,' I say, 'it would seem appropriate for anyone hailing from the Isle of Skye.'

'Why's that?' says Daphne.

'It may be like the Fairy Flag. When it was taken out of its box, disaster followed.'

'It would certainly take an expert to mend that,' Rena says.

'Oh, I could soon mend it,' says Daphne, reacting to the word 'expert'. 'That's nothing to me, with my domestic experience.'

'Could you really?' I say, loading my tone with admiration.

'Sure – no bother at all. Help me fold it up. I'll do it tonight and have it ready in time for Monday.'

We take it out by combined operation into the corridor and make an untidy parcel of it. To my relief, she carries it off at four o'clock. It is my first piece of luck since coming into the corridors of power.

Fairlie Brown is taking an intense interest in what he calls the Installation. By this he means not new wash-basins, nor yet a new heating system, but the new Headmaster. Fairlie will then be able to put back the responsibility where it belongs. He sends round a notice (please initial) to us all announcing the formal installation of the newly-appointed Head of the school, Mr Fergus Ogg, MA, BSc (Aberdeen). This will take place on Monday first at nine am and the Head will be introduced by the Provost of the Burgh, who is a member of the Education Committee. This is quite an inspiration on Fairlie's part, as it will obviate the necessity for him to compose a speech, and the Provost is right to hand, beside the lamp-post across the street.

I hear Fairlie telling Mr Gurney to see that the brass bell is well polished and the grass cut at the front of the school, as well as having the flag in position at the appointed time. Mr Gurney's usually ill-tempered face is suffused with suppressed rage, born of insult to his always immaculate bell, along with defence of his rights as a janitor to have the gardeners employed by the Education Committee to do menial things like cutting grass.

Mrs Whyte comes in today bearing a large parcel of such unwieldy dimensions that it can be none other than the flag. But she cannot display it in the staffroom unless it were to be draped from wall to wall. So we all go along to Ailie's room before the bell rings because this room has the largest floor space. Daphne, two spots of animated vermilion on her white cheek-bones, begins carefully to unfold it. Part of what looks like a tree appears, which once, forty years ago, must have had leaves that were green. All round the tree, species unknown, are little round objects apparently falling off the tree. Under it is a ship sailing along pursued by shoals of fish. All these allegorical devices are in one uniform shade of greenish-brown.

We cannot decipher the meaning of the strange device as we cannot lay it flat, but, by draping the folds over the desks, we see a kind of indeterminate composition building up. There is lettering, once maybe gold, along the top, and now truncated into three words where some stitches are – 'little corns grow.'

'What does it say?' asks Marjorie.

'I know!' says Ailie. 'Great oaks from little acorns grow! It must be an oak tree, of course!'

'What's the tree doing on the sea?' asks Vera.

'Little corns grow!' says Rena. 'We can't possibly put that up the flagpole. Suppose Fergus Ogg has bad feet!'

'Oh, nonsense!' says Daphne. 'Nobody could possibly read it flying up there.'

'What's happened to the other words?' asks Rita.

'There was a huge tear,' says Daphne, 'at the bit where "great

73

oaks from" was, and when I pulled the tear together, these words disappeared.'

'I'm afraid,' I say, 'we can't really put that up. It would disintegrate in the first breath of wind, and come down on the top of – the Provost perhaps.'

'Of course you can put it up,' says Daphne. 'And be sure to tell Mr Fergus Ogg, MA, BSc, who mended it for him.'

'We'll leave the decision to Fairlie Brown,' I say, inspired.

I refuse to do any explaining to Mr Gurney, so we all carry the flag along and leave it on Fairlie's desk.

I am sorry not to be there when he finds it.

We never learn of Fairlie's struggles either with the flag or in making his decision. But we do learn that a Union Jack has come to light from a cupboard in the Head's room, and that the janitor is now mollified enough to believe it is not beneath him to hoist this substitute.

After having told all the classes to come well-scrubbed, combed and polished on Monday morning for the sake of impressing their new Headmaster, we depart thankfully for the week-end.

It is a still morning. The Firth is unnaturally calm and ships' sirens are hooting down river. The top of the school flagpole comes into view as I come up the hill. The Union Jack is aloft, but hardly streaming bravely for the occasion. It hangs limp and unresponsive, and seems as tiny as a pocket handkerchief.

When the school bell rings this morning we are all to remain in the front playground, weather permitting. Since the weather permits, we do this. Fairlie Brown tells all the classes to turn round and face the steps and the main gate.

The bell rings for a second time, a sort of signal, I suppose. As it does so, the Provost emerges from his villa across the street. He is a small thin man with a small thin face and narrow shoulders. He seems enveloped in his suit of clothes, and I think it is as well that he is not wearing his robes today. The only thing that sets him off as a Provost is his chain of office, and even this hangs farther down his front than it does on most Provosts. It glints

74

brightly in the morning sun. But the ceremonial chain cannot increase his stature by one cubit nor bring him nearly up to the height of the impressive figure striding along beside him.

I draw in my breath and take a hasty glance at the other members of Staff. Their heads seem also to be turned to look in my direction, and I feel they are regarding me as if I were the Brahan Seer. For if this is Fergus Ogg, then he is indeed wearing a kilt.

He strides along beside the Provost, who takes three steps to his one, and who looks like a pet toy poodle beside a St Bernard. And, as if he were a poodle, Gurney's black Labrador rushes out through the crowd of children, runs down the steps and salutes the ornamental lamp-post as if to set seal on the occasion. The tiny procession is dignified enough to ignore this behaviour, and ascends the steps to where Fairlie Brown stands in his pin-stripe suit to salute them in his own fashion. I see a *sgian dhubh* in Fergus Ogg's stocking. I also see the Staff looking at me again. I try to concentrate on what the Provost is now saying to the classes. But, like himself, his voice is slight, and outside in the air it is carried away up to the heathery hills.

I spend the remaining uncomfortable minutes trying to keep the infants from fidgeting, and at the same time trying to get a better look at Fergus Ogg. He is a large man with very close-growing curly black hair which comes rather far down his forehead and ears. It gives him a strong bull-like appearance. His brows are well-marked and his hairy legs are like a caber-thrower's. His shoulders are wide and the breadth of his hodden-grey jacket seems immense. His complexion is sun tanned, and altogether he should inspire respect from the school population.

The final words of the Provost float over to me as he draws near the end of his introduction –

' – Degree from the University of the North, Aberdeen – '

I say to myself, 'Degree from Aberdeen, pedigree from Aberdeen-Angus.'

Fairlie Brown is now speaking, holding up both hands for silence. He shouts: 'All quiet for Mr Ogg!'

Mr Ogg makes no harangue. He is shaking hands with the

Provost as the big Labrador bounds playfully up to him. He pats its mighty head in fellowship.

He turns to the school and his voice booms out:

'A half-holiday today! How's that?'

An immense cheer goes up. Fergus Ogg has arrived – on the right note.

Mr Ogg, or, as he is sometimes called by the pupils, Mr Odd and even Mr Egg, is found by both Staff and children to be extremely approachable, so approachable, indeed, that there is always a queue of supplicants outside his door in the morning, which seems to be the chosen time for presenting petitions. Apart from the disadvantage of my never having any time to wait in queues, I scorn to clamour for his attention on the plea that he should be allowed to settle in without everybody asking favours.

Daphne Whyte has already asked him for a different stage of class for next session, although she has been no more than a year with Primary Five.

'Nobody should be kept at one stage all the time,' she asserts loudly. 'You get stale.'

If the same applies to staffroom presence, I should agree with her.

'It's the wrong time to ask for favours,' I say. 'You should let the poor man get acquainted with his school first.'

'If I don't ask, somebody else will, and I'll be stuck with that awful Primary Five for another term. Worst lot I've ever had.'

'The next lot may be no better.'

'Anyway, he was very sympathetic, and I've to get consideration.' And she goes on, 'Of course, when you've been married, you know how to manage the men.'

I have to smile at this without altering the set of my face, for Vera has told me that Mrs Whyte, in her two widowhoods, has gained and lost not only two husbands but also two stepsons from her first husband, and one stepson and one step-daughter from her second. All of these fled from the wicked step-mother as soon as it was humanly possible. In spite of which, she never tires of boasting about their success in life.

'I don't believe she even knows where they all are,' Vera had said. 'The research scientist is her favourite boast, although I'm told he hasn't been home in two years.'

Fairlie Brown has been doing some approaching, too, and he also is considered sympathetically. I can think of no more magnanimous man than Fergus Ogg, and I hope he won't regret it. Fairlie wants a day off to flit up-County where he has just bought a house. Promotion should be easier up-County because that is nearer to the seat of Administration. Or so Fairlie reasons, and this is very unreasonable and out-of-date nowadays. But I wonder if, privately, Fergus Ogg may be pleased to promote Fairlie's removal – and not only of his house contents, for I have discovered that Fergus has two phobias, noise and disorganization.

Ailie Chapman has been to see the Head to present an application – for a change of room.

'I told him I just couldn't stand another term of pandemonium,' she says. 'He was very sympathetic.'

'The poor man!' I say. 'How can he be expected to please everybody?'

I decide to refrain from petitions, although I could think of a few. But I definitely will not apply for days off, which is unbecoming in a responsible Head of Department.

Rita McGarvey comes in and announces her hopes of getting off for her cousin's wedding.

'I think it's absolutely ridiculous,' I say. 'He can't be expected to take everybody's class while the teacher goes gallivanting.'

'As a matter of fact,' says Rita, 'he's pleased to take the class. He says he gets to know the kids that way, and that makes a nice change from the last Head we had. Heads are having less and less time to do any teaching. Becoming sort of superior officeboys.'

'And not always so superior,' says Vera.

'I'd like to see him undertaking to teach the Infants,' I say.

I receive a letter today from the Head of Garlock St requesting my presence at a presentation. I left Garlock St in such a hurry that no presentation could be made. A cheque is enclosed, and I am asked to purchase something I would like to have and deliver it to Garlock St, so that I can be formally presented with it at a function to be held in *The Golden Anchor*, the town's one hotel. This function will include certain other presentations to other members of Staff and will take place in the last week of term at two-thirty in the afternoon.

I go along, petition in hand, to request a half-day off. I carefully choose a time in the early afternoon when the queue has dwindled to one boy with a slight cast in one eye. Mr Ogg is dealing with his petition on the doorstep. The request turns out not to be so much a petition as the laying of information about one of his enemies, who apparently climbed the Provost's lamp-post and placed his – the Clipe's – cap on top of it. The Head asks the Clipe his name. Francis Gillogaley – the boy with the bus-washing mother, of course.

I am generously granted leave for the afternoon.

'I'll come along and take your class at two pm,' he says.

'But will you really want to stand in for a class of Infants?' I say. I have brought them in during the afternoons for the last few weeks in order to break them in for the whole day next session. 'I could easily let them go for an afternoon, if you give permission, or get Marjorie to – '

'No, no,' he says. 'I'd like to.'

'But – '

I hardly like to say outright that I think no man is really qualified to take classes of Infants – least of all Headmasters.

'Don't worry,' he says easily. 'I had the forethought some years ago to take my Infants Mistress Certificate.'

I leave Fergus Ogg teaching Primary One AB how to make a rocking-horse that will really rock – out of toilet roll interiors and coloured wool and cardboard – and depart for *The Golden Anchor*. I expect that now that fish is de-rationed and Devonshire cream is back, and the five-shilling limit of charge for restaurant meals is relaxed, the meal we are to have will be an improvement on those offered during the last five years. Everybody has had salary rises over the past five years too, although expenses seem to be keeping pace. Five presentations! I am thankful I am one of the recipients today.

The others turn out to be Miss Munro, the Infants Mistress, and Bella McSkimming, who are both retiring; Miss Grott, who is being transferred to one of the newly-built schools; and Bet Dodd, who is to be married – to a Minister. With my promotion, we have run the gamut of reasons for leaving.

I wonder what the others will have chosen for their gifts. For myself, I have bought a handbag with a view to carrying home in it that handsome £35 responsibility payment that I get up at Heatherbrae for bearing all the stresses and strains of the past month. This £35, of course, looking even less opulent after PAYE, must be divided by twelve before it is put every month into the handbag, so that the extra weight is negligible.

The men teachers are always complaining about their salaries and the women are always suffering, but not in the deep silence of the past. The men are still paid more than the women for the same work, although 'same work' is an exaggeration, since, if the men ceased to teach in the schools tomorrow, education would survive, whereas, if the women all downed their pointers and dusters, the system would collapse.

Thus musing, I reach *The Golden Anchor*. The dining-room somewhat resembles an auction sale with all the gifts displayed on a table, which is, however, made more gracious by vases of flowers at either end. Every woman has a new dress, a new perm and a new hat, whether she is receiving one of these gifts or not.

Whereas in the past, chiming clocks and gold watches were the priorities of choice, today seems to be the era of easy chairs, table-lamps and handbags. Maybe there is psychology here: in the past everybody was the slave of the bell, nowadays everybody is exhausted and needs somewhere to flop. The only one who is different is Bet Dodd, who has chosen an attaché case, to carry her Diplomas about in, she says. Her latest is one for Arabic, she says, to be upsides with her Minister for Eastern promise.

Miss McSkimming has her own variation on the theme, her choice being a *chaise longue*, whereon she can elevate her varicose veins and ease her slipped disc, which she believes are occupa-

79

tional hazards. Miss Munro takes her standard lamp, and the Head recites her biography which is long enough for publication in book form. I take my handbag, lined with chamois, and with two interior pockets, in one of which I find a silver threepenny-bit for luck.

Miss Grott takes a brush set, which Bella says is symbolic of a clean sweep of all the old Staff of Garlock St.

Everybody has a generous glass of sherry, and we toast the end of an era. Besides the end of the era, it is mercifully also the end of the term, at the end of the week.

August
1950

I visit the school a fortnight before the term is due to begin. This is true professional zeal, but I am eager to have a good start this time. Nothing will be omitted that organization can achieve.

I think of Fairlie Brown's assurances that everything will be done. There will be no old sink, gas cooker or decrepit desks this year. There will be new cupboards to hold that £100 largesse of stock. And to enrich the environment still further, I carry, somewhat awkwardly, three geraniums in a basket.

The school is unnaturally silent as I go in. It has a queer smell. Antiseptic sawdust? What's this? Pails, brushes, mops all over the cloakroom in wild abandon – big cartons piled up in the wash-basins. I open the classroom door. Everything is just as it was – the sink, the cooker, the old desks, except that more cartons are piled up on them too. The only sign of any interest having been taken is the scrubbed floor. I have never seen it scrubbed before to such a state of bleach. Numbers of ominous 'skelfs' of wood stick up all over it like crocodiles' teeth.

I stand among the ruins and weep. I am almost in full retreat when I hear a swishing. Through a door leading from the back playground comes a man in wellington boots, dragging a hose.

'It's a fortnight yet before the school opens,' he says.

'I know that,' I say. 'Where's the janitor?'

'Right here,' he says.

'But Mr Gur – '

'Oh – him? He's away. I'm the janitor now. I'm Bernard – Barney for short.'

'Bernard what?' I ask.

'Mr Bernard, that is,' says he.

'I'm the Infants Mistress. How do you do?'

'How do *you* do?' he says. 'Are you new as well?'

'I suppose you could say that, although I feel aged today – after seeing this place even worse than it was when I left six weeks ago.'

'Oh – dinna fash yersel', hen,' says he cheerfully. 'I'll have it all ship-shape before ye come back. It's aye like that up to a week before they open.'

'Is it?' I say. 'But what about the improvements we were to get?'

'Your sink's to go tomorrow and the new one'll be in before the end of the week. So will the cooker – '

'That's leaving it a bit late, don't you think.'

'If ye hadna come up today, you wouldna hae known ony better.'

'True,' I say. 'And what about the new cupboard?'

'It's in my furnace-room till I get all this corridor cleared. Don't you worry. I'll put away your new stock in it.'

So that I'll never be able to find anything in it, I think, bitterly. But he seems an improvement on Gurney.

'What happened to old Gur – Mr Gurney?'

'Between you and me, miss, he was eased out, as you might say. Seems the new Master had complaints.'

'Really?'

Fergus Ogg seems to have achieved at least one success of 'easing out' in a short space of time. What other success of easing out might he not have achieved by this time next year? I could think of one or two.

'It'll all be ready a fortnight from now, miss – decks cleared, steam up and we'll pipe ye aboard as if you were an Admiral.'

'You been in the Navy?'

'Torpedoed in 1942. Here – give me them geraniums. I'll see they're watered and in your room on opening day. I've a wee garden o' me own, so I take an interest.'

'Thanks,' I say.

He picks up the geraniums from the basket, and, as he carries them off, I notice he walks with a limp.

A man of some sense, I think, a fact just as important as new desks and sinks. And undoubtedly the man to enlist on your side.

August, 1950

Today I have my first enrolment of beginners. I approach it with a combination of apprehension and curiosity. As I draw near the school, I think of my old Boss, in Garlock St's Infant Department, Miss Munro, and her imperturbability in the face of enrolments. I decide to be both gracious and impartial in interviewing parents and offspring. I shall be full of friendliness, yet firm in all contingencies. At any rate, I shall reach the school in good time, as it is now only eight-fifteen am. There will be time to arrange my appearance, time to set out my new notebooks and pens on my new (I hope) desk, time to receive any instructions from Fergus Ogg, on whom I want to make a good impression. And this will be done in the full quiet before a single parent appears on the scene.

I enter the school by the door on the left. Immediately I am plunged into a milling crowd of mothers and children, all jostling and impeding progress. I try to penetrate the crowd with 'excuse me' here and 'excuse me' there. Behind me more women have come in, so that I cannot retreat and try to gain entry by the other door.

'That's her!' I hear as I finally push ruthlessly through. 'That's the Headmistress.'

'Ask her, then – '

I press more determinedly through.

'I'm first, miss,' I hear someone say. 'Been here since eight.' Breathlessly I reach the staffroom. All the eyes that seared me have somehow wrought havoc with my carefully tailored appearance. In the mirror I look red and dishevelled. In the refuge of the empty staffroom I am combing my disturbed hair when I hear a knock on the door. Let none invade here!

Fergus Ogg follows the knock. 'So you're here!' he says.

'I feel as if I had left bits of me out in the corridor,' I say.

'Yes – it's a mob, isn't it?'

'I didn't realize there would be so many.'

'That's what I want to see you about. There will be a record enrolment this year. Not the so-called Bulge as yet, but a large number of families have been moved into the new council houses that have been built behind the school. They're really in the Homeston district of Greeninch, but there's no Greeninch school near enough to take them all, except this. Although we're not actually in Greeninch, still they've got to come here. It's all the one Authority, of course. As a matter of fact, I had little information about it all, and the list of eligibles has only arrived on my desk this morning.'

'Where are we to put them all?'

'Hitherto this school had well below its complement. So, if each room has its full complement, we ought to manage. Once it's sorted out, we'll maybe not have so many. Lots of the parents out there may not live in the streets from which we are to take the children. And they're all panicking in case they don't get in.'

'Scarcity creates demand. Nice change from the days when they'd do anything not to send them.'

'Yes, isn't it? There will also be enrolments further up the school, of the other brothers and sisters, but I'll attend to that.'

'Thank God for that!'

'There will be some who'll therefore try to gain admission on false pretences. There are some who should be in the nearest

Homeston school, and there are some who should be here. So admit those who are on the list of eligible streets and refuse those who are not.'

'I'll have to interview them in the classroom,' I say.

'We'll go there now and get you settled,' he says.

'I'll need an armed escort,' I say.

We go out into the noisy corridor, but the crowd of women falls away in front of Fergus Ogg, who cleaves a way with his mighty form while I follow in the vacuum thus created. We reach my classroom, and Fergus takes a chair, puts it against the door and sits on it.

'Nobody will get in now until you're ready,' he says.

But I am paying less attention to what he is saying than to looking at my room. The old dual desks with the clamps are gone. The floor has been repaired and smoothed, and sets of neat tiny desks with matching chairs are set in tidy rows. I make a note to try an arrangement other than the out-dated tidy rows. A new sink, gleaming white, is in, and the old cooker, glowering black, is gone. My three geraniums, in full flower, are on the windowsill. A new teacher's desk-table, smelling of fresh varnish, is there in place of the old mottled and scarred one I left in June. The chair that goes with the desk has actually a padded seat! And I am glad to see that the high chair that went with the old desk has not yet been removed. I make a note to retain that, as we need it for story-telling. It is the one relic that I can tolerate.

'What do you think of all that?' asks Fergus.

'Barney – I mean Mr Bernard – said it would all be done in time. I scarcely believed it. It's wonderful!'

'Your stock is all in your cupboard. Barney did that too. Barney,' he says, 'is the world's wonder. I shouldn't be surprised if he isn't some day acknowledged as the Head of the school. There are new wash-basins too.'

I laugh a little hysterically. All this time I have scarcely had time to realize that this is somehow a different Fergus Ogg today. By that I mean that he seems no longer the resplendent figure in Highland dress who took the school by storm of approval at the end of last term.

I think it has something to do with the suit he is wearing. It is a grey lounge suit which he has never worn before. It does not have the effect of making him look like the ordinary dreary run of Headmasters. Nothing could do that. But it has the effect of making him look like a ploughman in his Sunday best. His big muscles seem to bulge at the shoulders, and the trouser legs and the jacket seem just a shade too tight. Maybe he has put on weight in the holidays. To complete the bucolic effect he wears a pair of thick-soled brogues that clump on the wooden floor.

He puts the lists of entrants on my desk and says:

'I'll go now and see if I can form a queue of parents in the playground at the back.'

I remain marvelling at the room after he has gone. Truly, there is no more inspiring sight than an efficient and enlightened Headmaster. Unless, of course, it be an efficient and enlightened Infants Mistress.

I open the door five minutes later and the corridors are cleared. Murmuring noises filter in from the back door where the queue is revving up. I go back and lay out my notebooks and pens on the fair face of my new desk. I set a chair on the other side of it to hold the first ever of my applicants for enrolment.

Most of the confidence inspired by Fergus Ogg evaporates when the first to come in through my door is the belligerent Mrs Gillogaley, with a well-grown boy. All the Gillogaleys are well-grown, like their mother, who I see has this time abandoned her dungarees in favour of a voluminous tweed coat. She still wears a headscarf under which are bumps which I suspect are curlers. I could hardly expect Mrs Gillogaley to make more than one concession to convention.

I begin my enlightened tactics by indicating the chair.

'Do sit down, Mrs Gillogaley.'

'I'll staun,' she says. 'This is Sammy. Where'll he sit?'

'I'd like to see his birth certificate,' I say.

'He's five last Tuesday.'

'I'm supposed to see his birth certificate.'

'I've no' got it. I ken when he was born.'

'It's the rule, Mrs Gillogaley.'

'The last teacher took my word for it.'

'Oh, I'll take your word for it. But maybe you could send it up with Francis tomorrow.'

'Aye – all right – if I find it.'

'Is there anything you'd like to tell me about Sammy?'

'You'll find oot soon enough. He's feart, for a start.'

'Frightened! Of what?'

'Feart o' coming to the school, efter what his brothers have suffered.'

'What was that?'

'Aye gettin' the belt they are – frae that Mr Brown.'

'If you have a complaint about Mr Brown, maybe you should have a word with him.'

'I've had plenty o' words wi' him and none any good.'

'Sammy will be home today shortly after twelve o'clock,' I say finally.

Then – 'Oh, by the way, has he shoes for Gym?'

To my surprise she dives into a capacious bag and brings out a new pair of sand-shoes.

'Sammy'll no' be neglected,' she says.

'That's splendid, Mrs Gillogaley. It's easy to see that you know what to do. And Sammy's looking very nice today.'

He is wearing what are obviously new clothes and is well-scrubbed. His hair is sleeked down with water. Mrs Gillogaley, responding to the blatant flattery, smooths down his hair with a proud hand.

'Will I send the next one into ye, miss?' she asks.

'Yes, thank you, Mrs Gillogaley. Good-morning.'

'Eh – Good-morning, miss.'

The door closes. I show Sammy his seat and provide him with a large sheet of paper and some white chalk. I have made, I think, at least a modified success of my first entrant.

The door opens again and this time a well-dressed lady in a smart grey coat and matching hat enters. She closes the door carefully and brings a little girl to my desk. The little girl has shining fair hair, well-groomed and cut in a round bob. The lady smooths it down with a hand as loving as Mrs Gillogaley's.

'This is Diane-Dora Ponsonby,' she says. 'My daughter.'

'Oh,' I say. 'Augustus's sister? Very nice.'

'Yes,' says Mrs Ponsonby.

I say, 'Hullo, Diane.'

'Diane-Dora,' her mother says.

'Diane-Dora,' I say.

Diane-Dora stands silent.

'Say "hullo" to the teacher, Diane-Dora,' says her mother.
Diane-Dora says, 'Hullo.'

'Have you her birth certificate?'

Mrs Ponsonby produces a white envelope from her suede
handbag and hands it to me. The father's occupation is stated
as 'Company Director'.

'Is there anything you would like me to know about Diane?'

'Diane-Dora.'

'Sorry. Diane-Dora.'

'Oh, yes. She can read already. Oh, and count pretty well. She
can write her name and address as well as Augustus. You'll have
no problem with Diane-Dora.'

Extraordinaries at either end of the intelligence scale are always problems. The only comfort is that they don't come in
dozens.

Mrs Ponsonby offers an immaculately gloved hand as she
departs. I settle Diane-Dora in a seat – with a book.

The next parent has a little girl too, who sucks her thumb all
the time I am talking to her mother. The mother certainly does
little of the talking, as she is a monosyllabic woman who answers
'Aye' or 'Aye-aye' to every possible question. Maybe the thumb-
sucking is a refuge from this limited background of one diph-
thong.

After her comes a Mr McCartney with a boy called Edward.
He has no birth certificate. He says that his wife, who is at
present confined with the next child, has mislaid it. He promises
to send it to me as soon as he finds it. He gives the boy's birthday,
however, as falling on Hallowe'en.

'Is there anything you think I should know about Edward?'

'Yes. You see, he tinkles a lot.'

'Tinkles?'

'Oh, yes. You know – wets the floor. You'll maybe need to let him out quite often.'

At that moment, this encouragement produces a demonstration of Edward's ability to 'tinkle', and his father pilots him hurriedly to the new toilets in the boys' playground.

The bell rings just then and I run for Barney and his antiseptic pail.

I look at the queue and it seems as long as ever. I feel extremely inept at this enrolling. At this rate I shall still be enrolling far into the night. I decide to forego my interval and continue. An immense woman with a tiny boy holding onto her skirt comes in next.

'I've no birth certificate,' she says in a conspiratorial whisper. 'Ye see, I'm no' a Mrs – I've nae man. He went off and left me.'

'So there's no father's name?'

'No, miss. I make up for both father and mother.' Indeed she does, weight-wise.

'You can still get a copy of the birth certificate, you know.'

'I'll think aboot it.'

The tiny boy looks as if he could be accommodated in his mother's pocket – like a joey. I almost laugh aloud when she does in fact give his name as Joe Finlay (his mother's name). He is a happy-looking dwarf with huge limpid brown eyes. He puts his tiny hand in mine unasked as I show him to a seat and give him a drawing sheet. His mother's final act is to place a large paper baker's bag on his desk.

'His morning roll,' she says.

The next applicant turns out to be nearly six months short of five years, and the next two are from streets on the unstarred list. The queue slowly shortens.

A woman of swarthy complexion and wearing brass earrings comes in next. Her hair is oil-skin black and lies sleek on either side of a middle parting. She wears a blanket shawl like a squaw's. The girl she has by the hand is a small replica of the woman, even to the earrings. But the girl refuses to come beyond the classroom door and hangs onto the handle.

'Sorry to be a trouble,' the woman says. 'She's shy.'

'So I see.'

'Not used to the town yet. Ye see, miss, we're tinker folk.'

She nevertheless produces a birth certificate carefully folded up inside a paper bag.

'Betty Burke's her name. We're in one o' the new council houses for the winter wi' my good sister, who's taken to the town. But we'll be leaving again in the spring. Maybe ye'll see that Betty gets her lines then.'

'Lines?'

'Aye. Ye write down how many times she's been at the school. I think the last Master said it should be 200. Be sure ye don't forget her lines.'

'I'll remember,' I say, and put a note in my book which has now quite an impressive number of personal dossiers.

Betty Burke, who may be anxious to go by the spring, seems reluctant to settle in for the winter, and her mother has to stay with her for a long time. The moment Mrs Burke eases her way to the door, Betty howls.

I go on remorselessly enrolling, or, like the tinkers, I'll be in for the winter. At last comes the final parent into a room now as busy as the beach on a Fair Saturday.

This parent is a fussy man, wearing a bowler hat, which he doffs ceremoniously when he enters the room, and he shakes hands after removing a pair of yellow chamois gloves.

'Ha! A full complement, I see,' he says. 'I'm Walter P Gardiner, and this is little Walter. You'll find Walter a very intelligent boy.'

At least I know now that I have two intelligent children.

'Very intelligent,' repeats Mr Gardiner. 'All my family are distinguished at school. First prizes every year.'

(Not second, like mine, I think.)

'Very interesting,' I say. 'Have you his birth certificate?'

'Certainly, certainly. I know all about enrolments. My wife was a teacher.'

He hands me the certificate. He is designated on it as a tailor. I am surprised. I had expected at least a barrister. I check.

'Are you still in the same occupation as it says here, Mr Gardiner?'

'Oh – yes, yes. Eh – yes, still the same. My father before me. Family business. But I'm a lay preacher as well. Been to the United States and all that.'

Walter stands silently by.

'Education,' says his father, 'is all. Nothing like a good education. It all depends on parents like me. Walter is to have the very best.'

'I'm sure he will,' I say, wondering if this is an implied compliment to Heatherbrae. But inwardly I shake. Precocity terrifies me.

'Do you know what I did for Walter before I enrolled him today?'

'What was that?'

'I took him yesterday to Glasgow.'

'That was a very nice day out,' I say warmly, thinking that the fussy little man is human after all. 'I hope you enjoyed that,' I say, turning to the child.

Walter still stands by, big-eyed and silent.

'As a matter of fact, I took him up to Glasgow University.'

'Indeed!' I say.

'Yes, I stood him in front of the big gates and said, "Walter, do you see that big building? That is Glasgow University. You, Walter, are to go there when you grow up. You're to go there to that big school called the University, and take a Degree, Walter – an Honours Degree – a First Class Honours Degree." '

It's then the bell rings in the wee University of Heatherbrae.

'How many did you admit?' is the question I am asked eagerly by the Staff, after I subside in the staffroom in a state of exhaustion.

'Thirty-six.'

'Thirty-six!' says Daphne. 'None of the rooms can hold thirty-six.'

She looks at me accusingly. 'You must have admitted all those from the housing scheme. It shouldn't be allowed.'

I can see that I am clearly to blame for upsetting the usual routine.

'I admitted those at whose names the Head had put an asterisk. So all complaints, please, to Fergus Ogg.'

'Oh, I'm not complaining,' she goes on. 'I just thought you maybe didn't know this school just can't take large numbers.'

'It will have to this time. And next year the Bulge will really begin.'

'I hope you haven't admitted any Gillogaleys.'

'Oh, yes. There's a wee Sammy – an attractive infant.'

'Attractive!' Daphne goes on. 'A Gillogaley? No Gillogaley is attractive.'

'Well,' I say. 'This one is. And maybe next time you'll enrol them and then you can tell Mrs Gillogaley that.'

'Daphne,' says Vera Brown, 'could never enrol. She hasn't the necessary certificate. Isn't that so, Daphne?'

Temporarily, Daphne is routed.

'Did Mrs Gillogaley come in her dungarees?' asks Rita.

'Oh, no – in a very respectable tweed coat.'

'I'll bet she had her curlers in,' says Vera.

'I think I detected some bumps under her headscarf,' I say.

'A disgusting fashion,' says Ailie Chapman.

'The last Infants Mistress had something to say about that,' says Daphne.

'What did she say to her?' I ask, thinking she should have had the George Cross for daring.

'I remember that,' says Vera. 'She told her she should come properly dressed to interview the teacher at an enrolment, and not have her curlers in her hair. Then she asked her why she wore curlers during the day, when other people did the opposite.'

I am amazed at the temerity of my predecessor. Certainly I have a long way to go before I should be confident enough to reprove a lioness like Mrs Gillogaley. But I am curious –

'What was Mrs Gillogaley's answer to that?'

'Her answer to that,' says Vera, 'was: "I like to keep all my glamour for night-time." '

After lunch I am free to pursue my organization plans but think it will take quite a long time to heal the abrasions of the enrolment. I go out of the staffroom when the bell rings and stand in the corridor watching my other two classes filing in for afternoon school.

At the other end of the corridor I see Fergus Ogg on the same ploy. As the classes file past him, I notice a number of children casting at him looks compounded of disappointment and surprise. The enthusiasm with which they greeted his kilted figure at the end of last term has given way to a look which seems to say they have been presented with a tabby when they expected a tiger.

He comes over to me after the shades of the prison-house have closed upon them.

'Perhaps you would let me have your admission lists sometime today,' he says.

'There are thirty-six,' I say.

'It's a large number. It takes up a lot of time on the first day.'

'It was awful,' I say. 'I hope there aren't any more. Some on the list didn't come. Shall I score their names off?'

'Oh, no. They may still arrive.'

'Will they really?'

'Yes, they could come in any day this week.'

'It's a pity some other way couldn't be thought of than having them all waiting for hours.'

'Some day,' he says, 'maybe enrolments will be done the previous term. Then they could all come up and get acquainted with the school in good time.'

'But wouldn't that be just the same – all coming up when we're busy?'

'Oh, no. I mean for them to come up in selected groups.'

'You'd better not suggest that. It's far too advanced, don't you think?' I say.

'I intend to suggest it at the next Headmasters' meeting.'

'Enlightened ideas like that,' I say, 'take at least twenty years to percolate.'

The non-arrivers have arrived. They are there lying in wait in the corridor this morning as I hastily rush by. I am stony-hearted and without an 'excuse me', I dive into the badger's sett of the staffroom.

When I emerge with the ringing of the bell, they pounce.

'The enrolment was yesterday,' I say.

When the classes are assembled, and I have collected all my as yet unknown thirty-six, I firmly close the door on them, and go out to face the mothers. They number six.

I breathe more freely when of the six I find four have no asterisks at their names, and that one of the remainder is nearly a year below school age. Withholding an urge to suggest she should be returned to her pram, I successfully ease them all out and feel strong enough to interview the last applicant.

She is a woman with frizzy hair of a very unlikely colour, and is dressed very fashionably in a swinging green coat. She tip-toes up to me on peerie heels.

'I'm real sorry, miss,' she says, 'at not coming up yesterday, but him and me don't agree about Patrick's schooling.'

'Don't agree?'

'No, miss. Ye see, his father's a Protestant, and I'm on the other side, you understand.'

'You mean you're a Roman Catholic.'

'That's right.'

'And what don't you agree about.'

'My husband wants the family to go to the Catholic school.'

'But I thought you said he was a Protestant?'

'So he is.'

'Then why – '

'Oh, miss, he thinks the education's better in the Catholic school than it is here, but I think it's better here. Ye see, it's a mixed marriage.'

I agree with her entirely about that.

And after the formalities have been complied with, Mrs Mullen departs in triumph and Patrick brings the total of my class up to thirty-seven.

Since no more supplicants arrive today, I add the name of Patrick Mullen to the list and go along with it to Fergus Ogg, thinking as I go that this year Primary One will not be two stages A and B, but one and only one, as the classroom will not hold any more. As it is, it is over the Accommodation requirements. I'm afraid that Shirley's class will have to be rearranged to accept last year's beginners, as I can no longer keep them in my room. Shirley has many fewer than I, so this should be feasible.

On my way to the Head's room, I have to pass the classrooms in which Ailie Chapman and Fairlie Brown teach according to their own style. I go past Fairlie's door in terror in case the soul-shattering noise of a blackboard being thrown about should assail my already frayed nerves. I still contend that it is a black-board, and since nobody really knows, it is as good an explanation as anything yet suggested.

I hurry past, but there is nothing but silence, an unusual and ominous silence. Not the slightest movement can be heard. Maybe the class is out at Gym. But through the glass door I see the fluid outline of figures. Then Fergus Ogg emerges from the room. He wears the grimmest expression I have yet seen on his good-natured face. I present my list and he takes it with but the merest relaxation of the grim expression.

Ailie Chapman, on the other hand, is looking much less grim than usual at the interval.

'Something unusual is going on,' she says, 'I have never heard a sound from next door all afternoon. It's the first time I've been able to teach for a whole afternoon for months. In fact, it is so silent, I could hardly get on at all!'

'I think it's because of Fergus Ogg. He's what you might call a "cure",' I say.

He is 'Fergus Ogg' to us all now. Somehow Mr does not fit

such a name. Although some of the children still maul it about, most find it is one word they can all spell.

'I hope he never gets another promotion,' I say. 'But he's just the very man who's likely to get one.'

'I wish we could see the last of Fairlie Brown,' says Vera, who still squirms when she is called Mrs Brown.

'The only hope for Fairlie is a transfer,' says Rena. 'Nobody would ever promote him.'

'Don't be too sure,' says Ailie. 'If I had a friend on the Education Committee, I'd bribe him to vote for him if he were ever to be on a short list.'

'If Fairlie went,' says Rena, 'we should have a really good school, now that we have got a fine new Head and a fine new janitor.'

'To say nothing,' I add, 'of a fine new Infants Mistress!'

September
'I think,' says Daphne, with her usual air of prophecy, 'that Fairlie Brown is going to be on the carpet.'

'Why?'

'How?'

'Two members of the Committee were in the school yesterday seeing Fergus Ogg about something. They came after four o'clock and they went into Fairlie's room.'

'Was Fairlie actually there after four o'clock?' asks Rena.

'Oh, yes,' says Daphne, 'so there must be something going on. Mark my words, something's going to happen to Fairlie – something unpleasant.'

'It's Cassandra you should be called, not Daphne,' says Vera.

'Who's that?' says Daphne to Vera's delight. Vera enjoys revealing Daphne's somewhat shaky erudition.

'Generally speaking,' says Vera, 'nobody's going to believe you.'

'Were you really here yourself after four o'clock yesterday?' says Rena.

'Certainly, I was changing my dress prior to going to Glasgow.'

'And you just happened to see men going into Fairlie's room. Could have been men from the Repairs Department,' says Vera.

'And his room would need repairs too,' says Ailie. 'It's like a bomb site. Everything's kicked to bits.'

'You say he's to be on the carpet?' says Vera to Daphne. 'What other evidence?'

'Oh – well – I've heard rumours about it outside of the school. He's to be on the carpet all right.'

'You surely don't call that scanty strip of drugget in the Head's room a carpet,' says Rita.

'If I've heard aright,' says Daphne, 'it's not the Head's carpet. It's up at Admin.'

'I can vouch for the one up at Admin.,' I say. 'It's two inches thick. I've walked on it – or should I say sunk in it?'

'And I prophesy,' says Vera, 'that's more likely to be the one Fairlie's to be on. It would be just like him to land soft.'

These conjectures become crystallized into fact when Ailie comes in to tell us that Fairlie is going up to the Education Offices this morning. 'And Fergus Ogg is taking his class,' she says. 'I'll get another chance to teach today.'

'I wonder what it will be,' says Daphne. 'You see, I was right after all. Will it be out-and-out dismissal – or just suspension?'

'When did you ever hear,' says Vera, 'of any teacher being out-and-out dismissed – especially a man? The women sometimes discreetly fade out if they are what you call "disgraced", but – '

'In a case like that,' says Ailie, 'I've heard they generally disappear to the north of Scotland.'

'Never,' goes on Vera, 'have I known a man to be given the sack. They can embezzle the dinner money or run off with the Infants Mistress – but dismissed, never!'

'I've a feeling, all the same,' says Ailie, 'that Fergus Ogg has lodged a complaint. Same as he must have done about old Gurney. Look how he changed that.'

'The Wizard of Ogg!' says Vera. 'I don't believe anything will happen to Fairlie. He'll be back in no time, throwing blackboards about.'

'I hope he's for a transfer then,' says Ailie. 'And if he isn't, then I'm applying for one.'

'It will be a transfer if anything,' says Vera. 'Nobody would promote him – even to save face.'

But this is just where she is wrong.

The devastating truth is that Fairlie is virtually promoted. We hear today that he is going to a Secondary school – and up-County too.

'He'll get a lot more pay in a Secondary,' says Rita. 'It seems unfair, but there could be a snag in it.'

'I hope not for us,' says Ailie. 'I hope he's not just there on approval, as you might say.'

'Approval!' Daphne roars with laughter.

'You know what I mean,' says Ailie. 'If he doesn't give satisfaction, he comes back.'

'Ridiculous!' says Daphne. 'Maybe it's to discipline him!'

'How's that?' asks Ailie.

'Well, the boys – and girls – in a Secondary will take the mickey out of him, I should think.'

'Do you realize?' says Vera, 'that we'll have to stump up for his presentation?'

'He should present me with something, after all I've suffered,' says Ailie.

'And do you realize,' goes on Vera, 'I'm the one who'll probably get the bouquet from the children?'

'The trouble with such a school as ours, which is a miniature,' says Rita, 'is that to get enough for a presentation at all, we've all got to stump up double. Think of that!'

'Here's mine now,' says Ailie, diving into her handbag. 'It's cheap at the price.'

Fairlie leaves today. Ailie is sorry the old flag is not available, as she thinks this would certainly be an occasion for hoisting it.

Fergus Ogg's presentation speech is like the oracle of Delphi, full of *double entendre* in its predictions. Fairlie is very affable to us, and easily the most affable from among the Staff is Ailie. Being the oldest, she is asked to hand over the tobacco pouch which Fairlie has chosen for his gift.

'It gives me the greatest pleasure – ' she says. He proudly displays his present from his bereaved class – a packet of Woodbines. 'Smoked out at last,' says Vera.

Our main concern now is who will be coming in his place.

We have no time for lengthy staffroom conjecture about who is likely to be appointed as First Assistant, before he is upon us. Another example of Fergus Ogg's efficiency, Ailie believes. He has the resounding name of Roderick Hamish McTavish. It looks as if he has been selected for his sporting qualities, which, of course, surprises none of us. We learn that he is a Rugby player, a rowing blue, and a talented boxer. We shall not feel insecure with Roderick around.

'Has he good qualifications?' asks Ailie, 'as well as – all these extra frills?'

'He's fully qualified, if that's what you mean,' says Rena, 'and more than qualified fisty-ways to deal with the Qualifying.'

'Rugby and rowing and boxing are not what would have been wanted in my day,' says Ailie.

'I believe he's played international Rugby,' says Rena. 'Puts him in the upper brackets.'

'My two sons were both Rugby players,' says Daphne, 'and they had trophies for boxing as well. They hung over the mantelpiece in our old Homeston house for years.'

'Have you still got them?' asks Rena mischievously. 'Roderick might like to see them.'

'Oh – the boys took them when they went to their jobs.'

'Ask them when they come back to visit you,' says Rena. Daphne suddenly becomes very quiet. Rita winks at me.

Roderick is introduced to us. He is about half an inch taller than Fergus Ogg, and is less than thirty years of age, I should think. He has red curls and a formidable voice and wears a Harris tweed jacket. I wonder if we shall ever see him in a kilt. In all respects, he looks one whom few would dare to flout. Beware, Mrs Gillogaley!

We are now more than ever convinced that Fergus Ogg must be a man of secret influence somewhere, or a sort of benevolent Borgia, considering the speed with which he has rid the school of old Gurney, Fairlie Brown, and my old furniture.

It seeps through to us that the Qualifying class has dubbed the new First Assistant 'Rory'.

'But,' says Ailie, 'he never gives any more than one roar, and the class are silent for the rest of the day.'

October
1950

Although my classroom has been refurbished, my other two class-rooms have still the old galleries. I have tried to see Fergus Ogg about this, but he has been busy with men from the Admin. Rita, whose classroom is near his back door, says that there have been comings and goings all week, and men looking at the top of the playground. There has also been a visit from a Physical Education man.

'I know him,' she says, 'because he taught Gym in my last school. He seems to be in the dictatorship now.'

'I hope it's not any more drill,' says Daphne, 'I've too much arithmetic and reading to make up for all those that don't know them when they come to my class.'

We ignore the innuendo here, but Rita, whose class she has received, says evenly:

'It definitely is more Gym. We're to have it every day. And

those whose classes are nine years of age and over will be out in the playground, rain or shine.'

'I'll ask for a transfer,' says Daphne, whose class is nine years of age or over.

We have all been hoping for a statement like this from Daphne for some time.

Rita's forecast is not quite accurate, but the real facts are even more unacceptable. A vigorous woman in white plimsolls, a turtle-necked white sweater and a short navy skirt is brought to me today by Fergus Ogg. Her hair is close-cropped in the old Eton style. He has an apologetic note in his voice:

'Miss Strong – to tell you about the new Physical Education plans.'

My hand is crushed in a grip like a man-trap.

Fergus says, 'I have already told Miss Strong about our lack of facilities. But she will explain how to overcome them.'

And he makes off and leaves me to withstand the moral and physical muscles of this formidable woman.

'No difficulty about space,' she says enthusiastically in a creditable baritone. 'All your desks and seats in this room are movable. Excellent! Move all the desks and chairs to the side, and you will have a fine space in the middle for objective exercises.'

'Oh, yes,' I say, 'but the janitor is not always available to move the furniture.'

'Oh, no bother. The children will do it.'

'Really?'

'Pile them all up at the sides of the room.'

'If it's only once or twice a week, we might manage it,' I say reluctantly. As a Head of Department, I feel constrained to agree with the management.

'Oh, no good twice a week. Every day. Every morning, in fact.'

'Won't it be noisy for those next door?'

'They'll all be at it too. I'll just have a look in the other rooms.'

'Ah!' I think to myself, 'the gallery rooms. These'll fix her!'

'Ah! Galleries!' she says when we go there. 'Easy to deal with those.'

I see a chance of my dreams being realized.

'You mean – you'll have them removed?'

'Removed? Dear me, no. All the children need to do is step out of their desks into the passages. It's wonderful the number of things they'll be able to do, each on his own little pedestal, as it were – '

'Like St Simeon Stylites,' I cannot help saying.

'What was that?'

'Oh, nothing – just a thought.'

'They can jump, each on his own step. They can run up and down the passages, round the room and change places – creep below the desks. They're all going to love it.'

And I'm sure they will! If it ever comes to pass. I look at Shirley. Shirley looks at me. We both look at Miss Strong in wonderment. At last she goes to the door.

'We'll send you some equipment,' she says. 'Now – won't that be fun? They'll all be able to play as well!'

'Playing to the gallery,' I say.

'Ah! Very funny.' She gives a masculine guffaw. 'Good-bye. Hope you have a good time.'

Shirley, Marjorie and I are not the only sacrifices to the Goddess of the Games. Her machinations bring Daphne out in a rash, and Ailie talks hysterically about early retirement.

'I couldn't stand any noise again from next door,' she says fearfully.

'Maybe the new First Assistant will start a resistance movement,' says Marjorie.

'From the look of him,' says Vera, 'he'll be all for the games.'

'And,' says Daphne, 'in order to get further promotion, he'll have to say it's just fine.'

A notice comes round from Fergus Ogg setting forth arrangements for the New Athletes. Among them is a strong (should have a capital letter, I think) recommendation to strip for Physical Exercises, the boys to their underpants, and the girls to their – underpants. Even Fergus Ogg seems to boggle at the good old-fashioned 'knickers'. All must have black sand-shoes, but no stocking-feet, no sandals, no bedroom slippers.

As a concession, the time has been restricted to three sessions a week only. I detect in this a resistance on the part of Fergus Ogg to the caber-throwing chieftainess we had last week. He has, it seems, metaphorically used his *sgian dhubh* to cut her directives. A groan rumbles round the staffroom.

'Nobody,' says Rita, 'can force us to do all this.'

'I suppose we'd better support the Head,' says Ailie. 'After all, he's very gentlemanly. I should hate him to leave. He's sure to get further promotion with his talents.'

'Maybe,' says Rena to Rita, 'after he's heard your class and mine going at it, jumping and bouncing about close to his back door, he'll apply for the very next job that comes along. I also hope that somebody from the Admin is in his room when we all start Gymming up.'

'They should build a proper gymnasium,' says Ailie, 'but I don't know where they could put it.'

Vera has been unusually quiet all this time.

'Do you know,' she says at last, 'about HORSA?'

We all look at her. 'HORSA?'

'What's that?' says Daphne.

'It sounds like a bit of Saxon history,' says Rena. 'Doesn't Hengist go with it?'

'Is it a new line in Gym?' asks Marjorie. 'Don't tell us it's another imposition.'

'Or,' goes on Vera, 'have any of you heard of SFORSA?'

'I suppose we all ought to know,' I say, 'but I've clean forgotten.'

'HORSA was mooted in 1947 when the school leaving age was raised to fifteen, and the battle for school places was about to begin.'

'You can tell me little about the battle for school places,' I say, 'after my first campaign at the enrolment.'

'HORSA,' says Vera, 'stands for Hutting Operation for the Raising of the School Leaving Age.'

'Hutting!' says Rita, 'sounds positively obscene.'

'*Hu*tting was what I said,' says Vera, 'not rutting.'

'Well –' says Rita, mischievously, 'it was rutting that must have caused the hutting –'

'Oh, very clever,' sneers Daphne, 'but what's more important is –what has all this got to do with us?'

'Don't be surprised,' says Vera, 'if all these men who were examining the top of the playground are intending to begin a hutting operation right there!'

'Let's hope they build a suitable place, then,' says Ailie, 'and that it's comfortable.'

'What about that other thing?' says Shirley, 'that "force" thing. Has it got anything to do with us?'

'Oh – SFORSA?' says Vera. 'That means School Furniture Operation for the Raising of the School Leaving Age.'

'Great!' says Marjorie, 'let's have SFORSA and take away my old galleries.'

'I should dearly like some new furniture,' says Ailie wistfully. 'I've never been in a school that had any. The teacher's desk I have now has been here since I was a pupil in that room myself in 1895. If that suggestion was made in 1947, don't you think it shouldn't be long until we get it?'

'Ailie,' says Vera, 'how long is it until you are at retiring age?'

'About five years,' says Ailie, 'but I can retire any time now if I can't bear it any longer.'

'Then, my dear Ailie,' says Vera, 'on the day you retire, if it's five years from now, the new furniture will be coming in as you are going out.'

The staffroom is a-buzz this morning. It is about Fergus Ogg and his car. Also about his nylon shirts.

'Did you see the car at the gate?' says Vera. 'A Morris Minor – one of these new models. I wouldn't say "no" to being taken out in it.'

'Fancy being taken out by Fergus Ogg!' says Rita. 'In fact, fancy being taken out by a Headmaster!'

'Teachers are more often taken in by them,' says Vera.

'I noticed last week, too,' goes on Rita, 'that he was wearing nylon shirts. They're expensive, I believe – and you mustn't boil them.'

'I see you're getting ready to marry him,' says Vera. 'But I'll admit you might do worse.'

'Maybe he's courting,' says Rena.

At this point Daphne comes in. 'There's a car standing at the gate,' she says. 'Is there an Inspector here today?'

'Relax! It's Fergus Ogg's.'

'Fergus Ogg's?' says Daphne. 'Imagine him having a car!'

'Oh, don't be dated – lots of teachers have cars now,' says Rita. 'We were wondering who he might be taking out in it,' she goes on, to see how Daphne will react. 'Especially as he's taken to wearing nylon shirts.'

'So that's what they're made of!' says Daphne.

'If you marry him,' says Vera, 'remember not to boil them.'

We have long thought that Daphne may have earmarked Fergus for her third experiment. Her hair has been hairdresser-styled of late, and her face-powder has stepped up a tone from the 1920 chalk-dust to a cyclamen shade.

'When you think about it,' says Vera, 'we don't really know very much about our Headmaster yet. In most schools, when a new Head arrives, everybody seems to have previously read his biography.'

'That's because most of them go from one promoted post to another, all within the same County,' says Rita.

'And that's why they're all so insufferably provincial too,' says Rena.

'You can't say Fergus is provincial,' says Vera.

'But he's said to have come from Skye,' says Ailie.

'As far as I'm concerned,' I say, 'he was from sky the first day I came here – an angel, in fact.'

'You're all a nosey lot,' says Rena. 'What does it matter where he comes from? It's what he does that counts.'

'I think it's important to know background,' says Daphne, as if she were discussing a delinquent on probation. 'In fact I think it's very suspicious that he never mentions his home life.'

I think the same applies to Daphne, but I hold my peace.

'He could live with his sister,' says Ailie, 'or maybe he has a housekeeper.'

'He could be a widower,' says Daphne.

'Or,' says Vera, 'he could be a bit more exciting, and be concealing the fact that he's divorced.'

'Maybe he keeps a mistress,' says Shirley.

'We do know where he lives, at least,' says Rita, 'for I saw his address in the EIS Handbook.'

'Did you really?' says Shirley. 'And where does he live?'

'It was Upcairnmoor – but I can't remember the name of the house.'

'So that's why he needs a car!' says Vera. 'He'll be travelling every day. Fairlie Brown did say that when he came here at first, he was in lodgings in Greeninch. But that was only temporary.'

'If Upcairnmoor is anything like Broadlaw Moor,' I say, 'I'd prefer to live in Greeninch.'

'At least we've something to investigate,' says Rita, 'not many schools have a mystery man for a Headmaster.'

'Sooner or later, the truth will come out,' says Ailie. 'In a school it's impossible to be a mystery. Meanwhile, let's allow the poor man the right to be remote in his spare time. Such a gentleman he is – always so considerate to me.'

'I'll be going to Skye for my summer holidays next year,' says Daphne, 'and I may hear the truth of the matter then.'

'If he can keep whatever secret he has till then,' I say. 'Right now, he's making no secret about this Gym business. So be prepared for the worst.'

October

The worst is with us. Red revolution is rife, not the least being the Infant Staff. Marjorie and Shirley are reduced to shreds organizing Gym in the galleries. I am reduced to fibrositis lifting all the desks and chairs on top of one another three times a week. Fergus Ogg is reduced to sending a written complaint to the Education Offices.

The result is that two men come and look at the galleries. Marjorie complains about the men. They walk in upon her without knocking at her door and with their hats still on their heads. They look round the room without a word to her, then disappear leaving her door open. Such bad manners, she says. I get no inkling of this intrusion until now, when they are beyond the range of my strap.

'Maybe,' says Shirley at the interval, 'they'll remove the galleries now – even if they don't remove their hats.'

But the intention, if it ever existed, is more sinister.

A timetable is issued by the pressurized Fergus Ogg, for us to take turns at a Drill Hall about half a mile away, which is in fact, the local Orange Hall, kindly hired to the Education Committee for the purpose. This involves a trek there and back (twice a week) complete with outdoor clothes, indoor shoes and apparatus.

A further recommendation is issued for the Infants Mistress to co-operate by having her sewing classes make coloured bands and bean-bags.

I issue the ultimatum today and supply the coloured cotton which seems to me heavy enough to make sails for schooners going round the Horn, and should stand up to perpetual throwing around the Orange Hall.

'What about the beans to put in the bags?' says Daphne.

'Maybe the children could bring some until I get time to lay in a supply for you all,' I say. 'Then you can begin at once.'

Today Daphne says: 'They've all brought broad beans.'

'Tell them to bring haricots tomorrow.'

'Must it be beans?' she bleats.

'Anything that will fill a bag,' I say. 'Try *pisum sativum*.'

'What's that?'

'Swanky name for peas.'

I lay in a supply of the appropriate peas, thinking that these are easier to obtain, and the teachers send daily for their needs. Daphne, however, continues to beg for more and more peas. I do not seem able to satisfy her greed for them. While I receive numbers of neatly-sewn, semi-filled little coloured bags in due course from the classes, yet Daphne's peas, I think, must be dribbling out at the bottom as the new supply is poured in from the top.

By the time we are ready to begin our pilgrimage to the Orange

Hall, I have a number of bands and bags to take with us, as well as the highly-popular balls, bats and ropes. We go today, loaded up as for a safari. By the time we are ready, ten minutes of the allotted Gym period has gone. I am interested to see what the 'facilities' will be that the Hall is said to have.

We file into an echoing building with hollow-sounding wooden floors, a construction surely dating back to the Battle of the Boyne. There is a very small hall and a platform full of chairs and an old piano. On the wall above the platform hangs a huge portrait of King William, draped with an Orange Flag.

Hopefully I have a go at the piano, but it sounds like a barrel organ, and is encouraged to syncopation by middle C and two of the black notes playing a bump instead of a note.

I lay out the apparatus proudly and they all dive for their chosen objects, which are mainly balls. Meanwhile, I throw open the window to let in new air to displace what has been left of last week's Orange Meeting. Down below I can see the traffic rolling along the main street. And down below not long after, I can also see ball after ball flying out of the window, to disappear for ever under the wheels of the lorries. I hastily close the window.

But the amount of dust is so great that I am forced to open the window again. Balls are prohibited henceforth, and ropes too, which stir up the dust. All that are left are the bean-bags, of which we are still short.

When we are all dressed and arrive breathlessly back at the school, passing Marjorie's class on the way, I hasten along to Fergus Ogg's room, while the indignation is still hot within me.

'It's worse than the galleries.'

'I'll go down tomorrow and see for myself.'

'Take along a gas mask then,' I say.

It is sewing after the interval. I send two children along to ask Mrs Whyte if the bean-bags are now ready – or rather the pea-bags. Surely by this time enough peas have been supplied. Sufficient time has elapsed for a whole crop to be grown.

The two girls come back staggering under a heavy carton. The bottom falls out of it as they dump it at my feet. I pick up one of the bags. It feels like a kilogram weight and is stuffed to capacity with all those unending peas. Each bag is a veritable cosh, destined to lay out flat anybody in its line of fire in the Gym. I return the consignment to Daphne with a recommendation: 'These will do nicely for use with your own class.'

I look to see if the first-aid box is suitably equipped.

Notes from VIPs constitute the main feature today. Very Irate Parents are reacting strongly to the recommendation for the removal of skirts and trousers at Gym.

'No girl of mine,' says the first note, 'will go naked, jim or no jim.'

The next says: 'My Bertie has never worn underpants, so he is not to take off his trousers.'

Mrs Gillogaley writes: 'It is immoral for my Sandra to show herself in her knickers, and I am writing to the Head of the Education Committee to tell him.'

Marjorie Black treasures one from a parent of a child in her class: 'Nobody is going to force Marjorie to take off her clothes in public.'

And finally: 'I object to Harry exposing himself.'

Every member of the Staff has received more than one note in this vein. Some mention Fergus Ogg as if he were the manager of a strip-tease joint. The objections are mainly from the upper classes of the school. In my department the root of the objections is that they cannot take off or put on their clothes or shoes without help. 'You can fix his braces and button his pants yourself if you want him to take off his clothes.'

And in effect, this is what I have had to do for a long time, as in the Infant classes we have been 'stripping' over the last month, because of edicts from Miss Strong.

Ailie Chapman collects the greatest number of notes. She sneakingly agrees with them, too. To her, Gym, poetry, music and handwork are not the essential services.

'Just frills,' she says.

'I suppose you mean the pants,' says Marjorie.

'We never had them in my day,' she says.

'Must have been cold without them,' says Marjorie.

'Oh – you know quite well what I mean.'

I have one other trouble which the upper classes do not have, the tying of shoe-laces. To avoid this insurmountable chore, they go to all lengths, the favourite one being avoidance of the problem by wearing wellingtons on Gym days, even although the weather is as dry as Majorca in July.

December
The tribulations of Gym are temporarily swamped in the ritual preparations for Christmas, which began in October. Otherwise the carols will peter out after verse one. In Heatherbrae with its intimate atmosphere Christmas is less of a penance, although Daphne and Ailie approach it with a compound of reluctance and martyrdom.

I am asked by Fergus Ogg to tell the Staff that they are bidden to a party in the staffroom, which he and Rory McTavish hope we shall grace with our presence. Later, I go back and find Rory in the private room. I ask if their 'guests' will be permitted to make the tea.

'Tea?' he says, as if I had suggested cod-liver oil. 'Tea? It's a Christmas party!'

'What, then?'

'Take your choice – whisky if you like, or maybe the ladies would prefer sherry?'

'But –' I am about to say that the school hasn't a licence, but I feel this is the wrong way to put it.

'Ha!' he says. 'You dare not drink on the premises?'

'Well –'

'And you wonder how the others will react.'

'Yes.'

'After all the kids have had their fling, and got sick on chocolate and drunk on Coca-Cola, and gone home to yet another orgy, Fergus and I are coming along to first-foot you all, and bringing our bottles, so you'd better –'

'Bring our glasses!' I say, inspired.

'I don't mind passing the bottle round,' he says. 'But sound the others about it.'

And when I do, it is the first time we have all been of one mind about anything. Daphne begins some careless talk about her raffish exploits with the RAF during the War. Ailie always apparently keeps whisky in the sideboard, just in case. Of what, she does not specify. I rush back to Rory with the news.

If Ailie has any qualms, these are diluted by Eau de Cologne, a gift from Fergus and Rory. The rest of us receive sophisticated bottles of various perfumes. Daphne always did think that Chanel created just the right atmosphere for her personality. Barney, who is brought in as a useful accomplice, says he sometimes wears Channel behind the ears, but always Crawford's Five Star behind his larynx.

It is a gay and innocent party, and nobody fails to walk undeviatingly down the road to the bus. My route down Broadlaw Moor with the Rev Horace and his port was a lot more serpentine.

'Oh dear!' says Rita, as we are leaving. 'We can't leave the empty bottles in the school bin. You never know who – '

'Leave that to me,' says Barney. 'Here you have a professional disposer, of both bottles and contents.'

'Awfully sweet of the Head and Rory to be so thoughtful,' says Ailie, who is marching along, carrying her Christmas tree like a mace. 'It was a lovely idea, giving us all individual perfume. What kind did you get, Vera?'

'Muguet du Bois,' says Vera.

'What's that?' says Daphne.

'Lily-of-the-valley,' says Vera. 'Suits my shy nature.'

'I can't think,' says Daphne, 'that either Rory or Fergus went into a shop and bought all these gifts by themselves. Do you think that maybe Fergus has a lady friend who chose them for him? Do you think she – '

'If he has made a note of which perfume each of us has,' says Vera, 'he'll know just where we all are about the school. Eau de Cologne, the Sub-Qualy; Chanel, Primary Five; Muguet du Bois, Primary Three. By the way – ' she turns to me, 'he seems to have fitted his perfumes pretty well to his Staff and his ideas of them. But we haven't heard what you got.'

'Temptation,' I say demurely.

March
1951

HORSA has kicked. The hutting operation has begun in the boys'
playground, exactly on the spot where so much looking has been
done. The hut is a very temporary affair, a mere shell of prefabricated material. Inside it has benches round the walls, and no
cupboards, so we still need to carry the apparatus. Its superiority
to the Orange Hall is doubtful.

It furthermore provides a dilemma. We do not know whether
to strip in the classroom and run 'naked' through the playground,
or strip in the hut and drape it all over with clothes. In the end,
we strip in the hut to the sound of teeth castanets.

The complaint notes are decreasing in intensity. Only Mrs Gillogaley holds out to the bitter end, and forecasts the complete
demoralization of her daughter Sandra.

Today it is the turn of my class for the hut. It is a wet clammy
west of Scotland day which makes wellington boots fully justified

for once. No shoe-tying problems today. The top-boots are ranged round the sides under the benches. Very tidy. The lesson proceeds too, with precision, and comes to its conclusion in good time. Then they dress.

A voice begins to bleat: 'I canna find my ither top-boot!' It comes from Charlie Taylor who always waits for someone to do things for him. I go over to encourage independence by exhortation, and find Jimmy Carter wearing two left boots. I search around, but fail to find anybody wearing two right boots. I do find Jeanie Porter wearing one big and one small one. Maisie Brown has put on one with a plain and one with a corrugated sole. Five have 'Charlie Chaplin' feet, both pointing outward, and another limps round in only one, looking for the other.

To me all the boots look different. To them the boots all look the same. I arrive at desperation pitch trying to match them all up. Outside I hear Mrs Whyte lining up her class to come in for the next lesson. She opens the door, puts her head round and says: 'We can't wait out here in the rain any longer.' After she has waited a further five minutes, she sniffily insists on coming in.

The hut is a milling mass of small fry and big fry. Desperately I shove a boot onto the waggling foot of the boy who has only one wellington, and shoo them all out. In the classroom I try again to match them up by laying all the boots out in rows. This takes until lunch-time. Tomorrow I shall have something to say about having names on, although this has already been said more than once. Everybody is at last shod, I hope correctly, and they disperse for home.

I go back with relief to lock up. Suddenly I catch sight of two top-boots standing together at the back of the room. Appropriately, they are two left feet! I feel like throwing all the loose papers out of my desk and running out of the school with an eldritch screech!

I have tried for over a week to trace the owner of the two top-boots. On the next wet Gym day, everybody seems to have his rightful matching pair. I feel this is a derisive comment on my organization. But I decide that if I do not find the owners after a fortnight, I shall jettison them in the janitor's bin. They insult me standing there.

April

Our Easter holidays have come and gone. Luckily there is no distraction in the way of an enrolment after this holiday. I am nevertheless called out of the classroom several times by mothers delivering children late.

'It was my fault, miss. I thought it was tomorrow that the school went in.'

Mrs Carter says, 'Sorrry, Jimmy and the rest of us couldn't get out this morning. The handle came off the outside door.' I could have told her that this excuse is as time-worn as sleeping in or going for the morning rolls. 'Ye'll no' blame him, I hope.'

For the next half hour we try to pick up the lessons where we left off before the holidays. It sounds like an old engine cranking up, we have so much repetition, and nearly everything has been forgotten. To offset this state of affairs, Maisie Brown brings daffodils, and Catherine Davidson brings tales, principally about Mary Puddick, who, according to Catherine, has taken a bite out of her bread roll.

'Just like Goldilocks,' I say. But I can find no proof of Mary's misdemeanour.

'I ken that story,' says Catherine. 'I ken the whole o' that story. I tell it to me Mammy.'

'Really?' I say. 'You must tell it to the class sometime.'

'Can I dae it noo?' asks Catherine, who is more Doric-minded than most of the others, who are now trying to be what they call 'polite', which gives their words some queer maulings. It is becoming quite the thing to ask out, not to the toilet, but to the 'bethrowm', which, being interpreted, means the 'bathroom'.

As I have the dinner numbers to check and the register to scan carefully because of the late-comers, I think that if Catherine tells

115

the story now, it will keep the class engaged very nicely until I am ready. So I settle at my desk.

Catherine is standing beside me, but she is so small that she will not be seen by her listeners in the back rows. I lift her up on the high chair I had retained from the old furniture. She sits up on it as to the manner born, curling her legs round the legs of the chair to maintain equilibrium. The class sits hushed in expectancy. I wish I could achieve this total concentration from the class during my lessons. Not since Dr Gregor has there been such a hypnotic calm.

'Go on now, Catherine,' I say.

She begins, looking down at their upturned faces.

'I'm going to tell ye,' she says, 'aboot *The Three Berrs*. Just you listen, then. Wanst', she goes on, and gives a big gulp, 'Wanst there wis a wee lassie and she wis ca'ed Goudielocks. Ye see, she had her herr hingin' doon in ringlets, and it wis ferr herr, and that wis why she wis ca'ed Goudielocks. It wis a wee bit like Diane-Dora's, ye ken.

'Noo,' (another gulp) 'this wee lassie lived in a wee hoose wi' her Mammy and Daddy. She wasna very good at daein' whit she wis tell't. Wan day her Mammy says to her, says she, "Don't you derr go inty that wood by yersel." But this wee Goudielocks, the daft wee thing, whit does she dae? Well, I'll tell ye. She went inty the wood. It wis kind o' dark, but on she went. Then she cam' tae a wee hoose.

'Goudielocks was an awfu' wee lassie for peekin' at this and peekin' at that. So she peeked in the windy. She couldny see naething, so what does she dae? An awfu' cheeky thing. She gaed inty the hoose. The thing she didny ken, though, wis that the hoose belanged tae three berrs – a Daddy Berr, a Mammy Berr and a wee Baby Berr – '

At this point, there is a knock on the classroom door. Outside I find the Doctor and the Nurse. I turn round gratefully to Catherine. 'Just go on telling your story.'

I am sorry to miss the rest, I must say.

The Doctor and the Nurse are to examine the entrants from our last enrolment as well as some children from both Shirley's and Marjorie's classes. By the time I have arranged for the older infants to be prepared, and go back to my classroom, Catherine is coming to the end of the Goldilocks adventure.

'She loupit right up oot o' the bed when she saw them three berrs starin' at her, and she nearly fell doon the sterrs gettin' oot o' that hoose. Her Mammy gaed her a good hidin' when she got hame, and pit her tae her bed, "and nae chips for you the night, my lady," says her Mammy.'

Catherine beams down at the class, who sigh in rapturous agreement. Then the hypnosis is broken, and a great wail comes from Mary Puddick. A large puddle is slowly forming below her seat. I send Catherine for Barney and his pail.

May

I come in a little earlier this morning to fill in some forms for the Psychologist which it will be impossible to do while the class is there, especially as this is again Gym day. I am surprised to see Shirley and Marjorie already in the staffroom, sitting at the fire and drinking cups of tea. Both are usually flying in at the last minute as the bell is ringing.

'Ha! ' I say. 'Been sleeping here all night?'

'That's almost literally true,' says Shirley. 'Marjorie was here at six this morning.'

'So you've both been out washing your faces in the May dew – after thawing it, of course? But the school couldn't have been open at six.'

'It was this morning,' says Shirley.

'But there's no furnace to be attended to. The heating's off.'

'Marjorie and I,' says Shirley, 'brought Barney up.'

'It was all because of Billy Gillogaley,' says Marjorie, who looks a little bleary-eyed and tousled, and she takes up the tale.

'I woke this morning about five o'clock – well, maybe a bit before that – and suddenly remembered with horror that I'd left Billy Gillogaley in the cupboard last night! '

'In the cupboard! ' I gasp.

'Yes. I told him to go and stand in it till I came back from seeing the class out, and I emphasized that he was not to move till I returned to let him go.'

'Billy's the one who's in Vera's class,' I say.

'Yes,' says Marjorie, 'but I have the boys for Handwork between three and four, and Vera has her own girls for needlework. He'd been a pest all afternoon – kept us all back so that the lesson was held up.'

'But surely he would run off when you didn't come back to let him go?' I say. 'And why didn't you come back?'

'One of the other boys fell in the playground on the way down to the gate, and three of his friends brought him to me to be attended to. By the time I'd washed his knee and fixed him up, I'd clean forgotten about Billy Gillogaley.'

'But the janitor or the cleaners would find him and let him out,' I say.

'I didn't think of that at five am. The more I thought about it, the worse it seemed. I just had to come back and see for myself that nothing awful had happened to him.'

'How did you get here?' I ask.

'I was lucky to get a workmen's bus about five-thirty. All the time I kept thinking about Mrs Gillogaley maybe bringing a case to court.'

'Oh, nonsense!'

'At five am it seemed reasonable. I came up to the school and the chains were on the gate. I could see nobody at the windows, and I didn't know where Barney lived. Then I remembered that Shirley lived in Rosetree Avenue.'

'She came ringing the bell about six,' says Shirley. 'I thought she'd gone clean off her rocker.'

'By that time I nearly was!' says Marjorie.

'It was as much as I could do to calm her down with a cup of tea and some breakfast, making it all in my dressing-gown,' says Shirley. 'I tried to explain that Barney must have found the boy.'

'And had he?' I ask.

'Oh, no!'

'Was he really there all night, then?' I ask, thinking myself about Mrs Gillogaley.

'I knew where Barney lived,' says Shirley, 'and we fetched him. But when he opened up the school – no Billy! And Barney did not remember seeing him either – nor the cleaners.'

'I think,' I say, 'that Billy left not long after the last tinkle of the bell yesterday. Maybe even before you did,' I say to Marjorie.

After each member of Staff has heard Marjorie's tale of disaster repeated as each comes in, we all go to our classes. I stand outside and watch Marjorie's class going in.

No sign of Billy.

'You see,' she says, her voice distorted by rising panic, 'he's not there.'

'He'll be late,' I say. 'Just go to your class and leave it to me.'

Leave it to me. That's one of the things that promotion means, taking some of the burden. I pray for strength to withstand Mrs Gillogaley whose indignation this time will be righteous, if by chance Billy has not put in an appearance at home either.

My class are singing *Onward, Christian soldiers* when there is an over-loud knock at the door. Mrs Gillogaley, a dragon in dungarees, shoots the first tongue of flame. But Billy stands beside her and this heartens me, as he seems without scathe.

'This place,' she says, 'is just like Belsen!'

'How do you make that out?' I ask as evenly as I can.

'Her in there kept my Billy in yesterday. Put him in a cupboard, that she did. And you don't think that keepin' a poor wean in a place like that isna like a prison. Well, I think it's like them German concentration camps in this school.'

'When did Billy arrive home?' I ask. This seems to me the key question. But she ignores it.

'I'm going to write to the Head of the Education Committee and tell him,' she says.

'When,' I persist, 'did Billy arrive home yesterday afternoon?'

'Long after he should,' she says.

'But when exactly?'

'I'm just going along now to see that Mr Ogg and tell him this school's just Belsen!'

'Did I hear you say you were coming to see me, Mrs Gillogaley?' Fergus Ogg has loomed up behind her. She swings round.

'Oh – there ye are!' she says. 'First it's my Sandra having to take her clothes off. Indecent, I call it. And now it's my wee Billy being pit in a cupboard.'

I explain the position to Fergus Ogg before Mrs Gillogaley can give him her heavily biased version. He takes Billy and his mother off to his private room to resolve the matter. I still hear her stentorian voice Belsening along the corridor.

Before we dismiss at lunch-time, Marjorie is put out of her misery. With his peculiar genius in cases like this, Fergus has extracted from Billy the confession that he had not waited in the school more than a few minutes after the bell rang. But he had not reached home till long after tea-time. In the uncharted interval it transpired he had gone to play on the forbidden railway line. This misdemeanour he had been too scared to admit to his mother, and said he had been kept in by Miss Black.

It was as well, Mrs Gillogaley had assured Fergus Ogg, that her Billy was a sensible boy who would never let himself be left in danger in a school all night, especially in one that was Belsen all over again.

I feel very grateful to Fergus Ogg for my rescue from Mrs Gillogaley. He comes along to see me later.

'You had better speak to Miss Black,' he says, 'about the inadvisability of putting anything in her cupboard other than her school stock.'

'I don't think she actually put him right in,' I say in mitigation. 'The cupboards are not deep enough. He was only behind the door.'

'Nevertheless, tell Miss Black to try other methods, and since she seems to have tried most of the more moderate ones, tell her next time to give him a touch of the tawse.'

'The tawse?' I say. 'I don't think she even has a strap.'

'That's right. He seems to me the kind of boy who needs some physical correction from time to time. His father pampers him, strangely enough.'

'It's the mother who seems to be the fighter in the home.'

'Probably. And this is all wrong according to Billy's sub-conscious psychology. It seems to him that he is not being treated like a male.'

I am doubtful about this reasoning, and wonder if substituting Marjorie for Mr Gillogaley is going to have much effect on Billy.

'Sometimes,' goes on Fergus, 'children will take meekly from the teacher punishment they won't take from an indulgent parent.'

'Well,' I say, 'we'll try giving violence where it is longed for, but maybe we won't be bothered again, although I doubt it.'

'And tell Miss Black,' he says, 'that I'd like to see her in my room at three pm today.'

I duly approach my assistant to deliver my first reprimand. How does one couch such disapproval? The intimacy of a small school somehow augments reprimands and quarrels, in the same way as it enhances sympathies and friendships. In a large school these things go almost unnoticed.

'You're to go to see the Head at three pm today,' I begin.

'Am I to be dismissed?'

'Of course not. You may be logged,' I say with sudden inspiration, as a preliminary to the reprimand.

'Logged?' Shirley's eyebrows go up into her hair.

'I didn't say flogged. Heads have to log incidents which occur in the school. Sometimes they have repercussions.'

'Repercussions?'

'Oh, I don't suppose this one will. Fergus Ogg dealt with Mrs Gillogaley, but her capitulation was not absolute. You mustn't on any account put children in cupboards, no matter how severe the provocation.' There! I had done it.

'And,' I add, 'you're to give Billy a touch of the tawse the next time he causes trouble.'

'The tawse?'

Marjorie's replies seem to be all monosyllabic repetitions today. But I can see she is preparing to dispute this recommendation with the idealism of the probationer all set to rule without the leather.

'Yes,' I say, 'but in moderation, of course. Remember he wants to see you at three pm.'

'To get the tawse?'

I am glad to see that she is now relaxed.

'Metaphorically – yes,' I say, 'in moderation, I expect.'

'Oh – but I don't possess a strap. Where do you buy one, and what do you ask for?'

'At a saddler's, and you ask for a Lochgelly.'

'Lochgelly?'

'It's a place in the Kingdom of Fife where straps come from.'

'Will it cost a lot?'

'It will cost you nothing this time,' I say. 'The last Infants Mistress left me two straps in her desk – one with four fingers and one with two. I'll let you have one of them. I seldom use them myself.'

'You see – you don't believe in it either.'

'I didn't say that. I believe in it in real moderation and according to circumstances. An old saying is, "Never use the tawse if a word will do." But if word after word will not do – then . . . Also,' I add, 'it's better to use it a little while naughty boys are themselves little, than to use it when they're grown bigger. It only brings resentments then.'

'They say that sometimes giving the strap does the teacher more good than the pupil,' says Marjorie, 'at least, that's what we used to say as students.'

'I've heard that said, and I suppose it's quite true. You let off steam that way. If it helps both, it might be justified!'

'Come to think of it,' says Marjorie, 'I don't think I know how to use it.'

I go back to my room and fish out the two straps from the back of the desk. I select the one with four fingers. It is a black shiny one that has the patina of a lifetime of disciplinary service about it. The one with the two fingers is a stiff, hard, uncompromising weapon, which strikes me as being its own master and difficult to aim. I go back to Marjorie.

'Here it is!' I say. 'So far there are no bits of flesh adhering to it!'

'Horrible!' says Marjorie.

'Now –' I demonstrate by taking Marjorie's hand. 'You must hold the wrist – thus – and with your other hand carefully bring the strap down on the palm – so –'

'Here! That was sore!'

'Ah, yes, you'll not repeat the mistake again! You can tell Fergus Ogg you got the strap from me, and maybe he'll hold his hand. Now you know how to do it, and if you don't know the technique by the next Handwork day with Billy Gillogaley, I'll send you to Daphne Whyte for further tuition. She's the best kid-walloper in the school.'

'The Lord forbid!' says Marjorie, putting the distasteful object in her desk.

'You can always practise on the wood of one of the desks,' I say. 'Fairlie Brown used to do something like that. And if the first clip doesn't subdue Billy, you can always try roasting the fingers of the tawse for better performance.'

'Roast!'

I leave Marjorie looking as if she had just heard of a witch's Sabbath. But – after all, if she were teaching in England she would use a cane, a thing we Scots think is so barbaric!

Marjorie comes in early this morning.

'Early again!' says Vera. 'Up at five, eh?'

'Got a lift this morning,' says Marjorie.

'Who from? I could do with one up that brae.'

'From Fergus Ogg,' says Marjorie.

'Hope it will be me tomorrow,' says Vera.

'He seems to be travelling from up-County every day now,' says Rita. 'Must be settled in up there.'

Marjorie hastens off to the classrooms with Shirley.

'You would think it was the first time she'd ever got a lift from him,' says Daphne.

'Well, isn't it?'

'Oh, no. I saw her getting into his car the day we went off for the Easter holidays. And they went in the up-County direction, too.'

'Could have been an abduction,' says Vera.

'Only a deduction,' says Daphne with unusual wit.

'And if you only saw the place he lives in – ' Daphne pauses tantalizingly.

'I take it that you have seen it,' says Ailie, who is not above encouraging a good gossip.

'I was taken for a car run in the holidays by some of my friends,' says Daphne, 'with the Provost and his wife to be exact. I'm very friendly with them.'

'And you went up-County?' says Ailie.

'Yes, we happened to go the detour by Upcairnmoor,' says Daphne.

'Who thought of that?' asks Vera.

Daphne ignores this remark. 'I realized,' she says, 'that Upcairnmoor was where the Head lived. The Provost knows the Head quite well, of course.'

'Did you call at the house?' says Ailie.

'House!' says Daphne. 'It's more like a castle – a big place with corbie steps and a tower.'

'Scots baronial is what you call it,' says Vera. 'But it sounds exciting. Do you think he might abduct me next?'

'What I say is,' goes on Daphne, 'what does he want with a big place like that when he has no wife?'

'Maybe she's mad and he keeps her locked up in the tower – like Rochester, you know.'

'Who's that?' says Daphne, characteristically.

'Oh skip it,' says Vera, 'but you know what we suspected – a mistress perhaps.'

'It's suspicious to me,' says Daphne, bent, as usual, on embellishing facts. 'I can't think why we have never found out any more.'

'Maybe there's nothing to find out,' says Ailie. 'All I know is that since he came to this school, it's been a different place. I don't care whether he has a dozen princesses locked up in his tower, as long as I can hear myself speak in my room. I hope that

Rory McTavish will continue as he has begun. Oh, by the way – I clean forgot – ' She turns to me. 'I've a letter for you. Sorry I didn't give it to you sooner. Fergus asked me to hand it to you as I came in.'

I glance at the signature when I open it.

I call after Ailie as she is leaving the staffroom, 'What was the name of my predecessor?'

'Miss Deans.'

'Jeanie?'

'No, of course not – Elizabeth Jane – '

'That's right, then. It's from her. She makes a rather unusual request.'

'What's that? She was a warmer, she was,' says Ailie.

'A warmer?' I say.

'A warmer of fingers,' she says. 'Was always walloping the kids – even worse than Daphne. I hope you'll not become like her. And glad to retire, she said. Hated every minute of it.' She looks at me expectantly.

'This letter asks me to send on her Lochgelly.'

'Whatever for? Is she going back to teaching? I shouldn't have thought she'd have darkened the portals again. Have you got her Lochgelly?'

'Yes, she left it in her desk. And no, she's not back teaching.'

'What then? What does she want a strap for if she's retired?'

'She says – I quote – that she wants it for "sentimental reasons".'

'Did you ever?'

'There were two in her desk. Do you know which was – was the – ?'

'The one she liked best?' says Ailie. 'It was a black strap. She always carried it in her overall pocket.'

'You don't say!'

I go along to Marjorie who looks as if I have undermined her faith in me, and I swap the one with the two fingers for the black one with the four.

Sentimental reasons? And will she mount it on her wall along with the Lochaber axes and the broadswords?

This is Friday afternoon, and there is depletion of numbers in the class. The best of the previous intake of beginners is now with Shirley, for since August all of us have two stages to teach. The Primary One B section, which I have, now do the afternoon session. Today there seems an unusually small number present.

Mary Puddick is off. Jimmy Carter is off, as is Sammy Gillogaley. They seem to think that when they stay off on a Friday afternoon, this fact will have been forgotten by the time Monday comes. Fergus Ogg is determined to stamp out this habit, which permeates the whole school. We have to send a list of the defaulters to him on Fridays. When the class is settled to reading their Red, Yellow and Blue Storybooks, I go along to present my list.

'Ah!' he says, 'another Puddick. They always hop off on Fridays. Has she been off all day or only this afternoon?'

'Only this afternoon.'

We suffer from a plethora of Puddicks. Every teacher has one in her class just now, except Ailie Chapman, who had one last term. There are, in effect, eight Puddicks, and the oldest ones are not necessarily in the highest classes, for some have been detained at one stage for as long as the teacher can possibly stretch the need for this. Academically, they verge on the handicapped, except, maybe, Marigold, the eldest, of whom something might be made, were it not for the weight of her demanding brothers and sisters.

But in the school this afternoon there is not a Puddick to be found.

Mrs Puddick has two more little Puddicks at home, lining them up for my future enrolments. She is a voluminous but amiable woman in a capacious tweed coat, and she wears bedroom slippers with sleazy fur surrounds as she trails to the school nearly every morning with the youngest, Mary, who would otherwise wander away to the swings in the park. While Mrs Puddick performs this duty, Mr Puddick remains in bed, where he composes long and amazingly literary letters to Fergus Ogg, the teachers and the manager of the Labour Exchange. He is seldom in work, much of his energy being employed in evading it, with some left over for a variety of questionable enterprises. Although his family shows little sign of academic prowess, Marigold has some of her father's enterprise for the questionable. She seems to have the additional one of organization.

'We can't do much today,' says Fergus. 'But I'll have the Attendance Officer visit the home on Monday.'

'It seems to be a popular superstition that on Friday afternoons we don't do very much anyway, so it's hardly worth going back.'

'I intend to alter all that,' says Fergus.

This is Monday. It turns out that it was no fault of either mother or father Puddick that their children failed to come back on Friday. And it turns out that it is Marigold who is the mainspring of the family's defection. This we learn in serial form, partly from Fergus, partly from the Attendance Officer and partly from the Sergeant of Police.

While the law-abiding pupils of Heatherbrae were engaged on Friday afternoon in what Ailie Chapman is pleased to call 'frills' – music, poetry, painting and handwork – the Puddicks, scorning culture, were being briefed for enterprise by Marigold. She, wheeling a high pram, was then on her way to Greeninch, followed by a string of Puddicks – Mary, Bunty, Jamsie, Glad, Bambi, Wattie and Elijah. Marigold remained outside the side entrance to Woolworth's in Molasses Lane, while the family infiltrated themselves among the crowded shoppers in the store.

Soon a total of thirty heterogeneous articles culled from the counters were secreted under the pram cover with Mary on top, as a result of the machinations of Mary, Bunty, Jamsie, Glad, Bambi, Wattie and Elijah.

The next instalment of the plot we heard four days later. Apparently the object of these endeavours was a Grand Jumble Sale held on the Puddicks' drying-green. Unfortunately for Marigold, Mr Puddick saw the advertising bill chalked out by Wattie, the artist of the family. He went to see what was going on. This curiosity of his happened to coincide with one of his rare moral moods. These take charge occasionally, and motivate him to produce his Bible. On a great wave of virtue, and clutching this Bible, he had marched the whole family down to the police station.

Sergeant Milne himself gives me the final instalment of the tale this morning, when he comes round to make more inquiries about the members of the family under my jurisdiction.

'Why do you think father Puddick turned King's evidence?' I ask.

'Oh,' says the Sergeant, 'to let us think he's on the side of the law. We are not deceived.'

'What did he say when he arrived at the station?'

'He stood and stormed at the family lined up at the desk in the station. He roared mightily at the poor wee things and shouted: "Pluggin' the school, were ye. Now ye see what comes o' pluggin' the school." '

When Sergeant Milne asked them why they had used the articles for a jumble sale, Marigold had piped up: 'Everybody's doing it – all the kids in the street. They dae it tae help cripples and things.'

'Was yours for cripples?' the Sergeant asked.

'Oh no,' said Marigold, 'oors was for the handicapped children.'

June
1951

Being a boss yourself is different from seeing somebody else being one, especially in a school where it only means adding a lot of extra chores to those you had as an assistant. Not having tackled these Combined Ops before, it was some time before I learned how to carry on teaching and at the same time to tour the school, visit classes, talk to parents, doctors, nurses, dentists, Speech Therapists and, of course, Gym enthusiasts, who never give up.

Each successive June during the last ten years in schools has shown more and more of Ailie Chapman's 'frills' taking over from what she calls 'real' lessons. We now can count out June from scholastic pursuits. Energies are poured into Shows of Work, Outings, going to the Church, Sports Days, and the culminating penance, the Prize-giving. Modern Headmasters go wild with inspirations for more and more of these events. This year Fergus

Ogg, whatever he may be hatching up for the future, limits his desires to the Church Parade and the Prize-giving, especially the Prize-giving.

There is nothing shows a Head's genius for organization more than a Prize-giving. The successful Head is he who can delegate. The former Head had failed miserably here, we have been told. Fergus Ogg is set on delegation, and he first delegates the seating arrangements for the Prize-giving to Rory McTavish, which is a master stroke for Fergus, as it is in the nature of a classical task like that set for the mighty heroes of Greek mythology. Rory's task is to find a way of fitting nine classes into two classrooms. These two classrooms are certainly the largest in the school, his own and Ailie's next door, but even with the dividing glass partition folded back, the space left presents a mathematical conundrum for Rory.

I am callous enough to agree with Daphne for once that he gets paid more for doing it than we should, or than we do for our tasks. For Fergus has doled out tasks to us all.

I am asked to see to the catering for the guests and Staff after the Prize-giving. This might turn out to be an even more exacting task than Rory's, as food fluctuates from rationing to non-rationing from month to month, and I can see myself searching out the local spivs and becoming a black marketeer.

My morals may be in danger, but my morale is suddenly given a great boost by an invitation from Fergus Ogg that elevates me to a seat on the platform on Prize-giving day. Marjorie calls it 'giving me my rightful place'.

I wonder how comfortable this place is going to be when I take a look at the platform in Rory's room, along the sea-edge of which the tide of nine classes will beat with corrosive force. Nevertheless, I think of myself sitting up there along with the élite. For the first time I shall see it all looking down from above rather than looking up from below, or rather half-looking from below, since hitherto I have always had my eye swivelled on the suspects in my class and a free hand ready to grab offenders of the social code.

Who else, I wonder, will be on the platform? Who will present the prizes? At least I shall not be required to make a speech: I am not high enough for that. But at least high enough to have a seat among the mighty.

The staffroom is rustling with speculation.

'Who's to present the prizes this year?' asks Rita.

'It was the Provost's wife last year,' says Ailie. 'A very nice lady – very genteel, I thought.'

'A friend of mine,' says Daphne, 'although the Provost himself is more – more considerate, I think.'

'She wasn't so genteel when Francis Gillogaley climbed their lamp-post – or about old Gurney's Caesar either,' says Vera. 'She came out with a pail and washed the bottom of the lamp-post, then put down chloride of lime. But it didn't make a whit of difference to Caesar.'

'And after that she got the Corporation to send a man to re-paint it,' says Rita. 'The school wasn't in very good odour, if that's the right way to put it.'

'Wonder who it will be, then?' says Rena. 'I can't see the Minister's wife being asked. The Minister's kids never get prizes.'

Marjorie comes in just then.

'We've just been discussing who's to present the prizes this year,' says Rita.

'Oh,' says Marjorie, 'don't you know? Well, I can tell you.'

'You?' says Daphne, in a tone which says she is having her worst conjectures realized.

'Yes – I came up just now in the Boss's car.'

'Headmaster's,' corrects Ailie.

'In the Headmaster's car, then,' says Marjorie. 'But maybe you'll not be interested to know, for he'll be sending round word about it today.'

'Oh, yes, we'll be interested to know,' says Ailie. 'But, you know, we always called the Headmaster by his proper title in my day, my dear!'

'Who is it?' says Daphne.

'I'm told,' says Marjorie, 'it's to be Lady McTaratan.'

'Lady McTaratan?' squeaks Daphne. 'But she's a millionaire!'

'All the better,' says Vera, 'maybe she'll buy the prizes.'

'She's the wife of Sir Alastair McTaratan,' says Ailie, 'and they own ship-yards and steel mills, and have a huge place up the County. They own great stretches of land with shooting-boxes and all that. I don't really think this school is important enough for her Ladyship to present the prizes.'

'I think,' says Vera, 'it's time this school was in the news and had some attention paid to it for a change. I'm all for Lady Mc-Taratan.'

'Quite right,' says Rita. 'I'll buy a new dress for the day.'

'Made of taratan?' asks Vera.

'I agree too,' says Rena. 'But how did Fergus Ogg conspire to get her to hand over the prizes?'

'Oh,' says Marjorie,' she's a friend of his.'

'Friend!' says Daphne. 'What kind of friend?'

'He goes to dinner parties at the McTaratan's,' says Marjorie.

'Of course,' says Rita, 'he has a house up the County as well. Maybe they are next door neighbours.'

'You yourself told us,' says Vera to Daphne, 'that his place is well-nigh a castle itself, so it's not so surprising after all.'

'What surprises me more,' says Ailie, 'are dinner parties at all. How can anybody have dinner parties on a ration of meat such as we have?'

'Not like we have,' says Daphne. 'I'll bet they know where to get more than corned beef.'

'Folk like them don't exist on rations. They go out and shoot hares and pheasants and rabbits or ducks. Use your imagination.'

'I must insinuate myself with her Ladyship,' says Rita, 'and maybe I'll get a brace of pheasants from the Castle.'

'Strikes me we don't know very much yet about our Headmaster,' says Daphne. 'After what happened last year in England about all those Communist Headmasters being banned – well, it makes you wonder, doesn't it?'

'That's absolutely ridiculous!' says Ailie. 'You don't hobnob with Lord and Lady This and That if you're a Communist.'

'I was only saying what I'd read about,' says Daphne. 'There's a positive wave of spies all over the world – very high-up ones too. Every day there's another discovered.'

'Now we know what his castle is for,' says Vera. 'Its dungeons are occupied by sinister chemists and physicists.'

'You're all talking nonsense,' says Ailie. 'I'm going to look forward to the Prize-giving for the first time in years, having all the arrangements done for me by Rory.'

'Lucky you!' says Rita. 'I've been given the job of playing the piano for the hymns – and there's so little space that I don't know what I'm going to do with my elbows.'

'Job!' I say. 'You shall hear about mine.'

'Yours?' says Daphne. 'I thought you were to be up on the platform with the aristocracy.'

'That,' I say, 'is a mere sop to my vanity. Actually, I'm to see to the catering.'

'Catering?'

'Yes. I've been steeling myself to tell you all. We'll need a supply of sandwiches and cakes.'

'Sandwiches! How can you make sandwiches with our meat ration?'

'We used beetroot mixed with dried egg during the War,' says Ailie.

'Revolting!' says Shirley. 'I'd think that surely Lady Mc-Taratan would send us a side of venison from one of her deer forests.'

'It's an idea,' I say, 'but, I fear, a fantasy.'

Finally we decide to divide the labour, each to bring a half-dozen sandwiches, spread with margarine, if enough available, but whale meat excluded. For sweet, to bake a few utility cakes, but mineral oil not recommended. Daphne offers a modest supply of tea and sugar, hinting darkly at a handsome black marketeer as one of her contacts. Ailie offers a luxurious hand-embroidered supper-cloth, considering it's for Fergus Ogg and his distinguished guests. Such good tone they will give to the school, she says, just as it used to have in the old days.

I go to tell Fergus Ogg about my success with the food arrangements, and he immediately overthrows all my plans. He will, he assures me, be providing an ample supply of all we shall need. All I have to do is lay out the food in the room allotted, where the guests will be served – if they survive the Prize-giving. There will, he says, be venison pâté, pheasant sandwiches, savouries, apple pies and a number of cream sponges –

'Up the County!' I almost shout as I rush back to the staff-room to tell the greatest news since 1949 when sweet rationing was abolished (for the nonce) and you could suddenly buy two Mars Bars to eat at one sitting. It is some time before we adjust to the idea of such prodigality.

Who else will be having a place on the platform beside Sir Alastair and Lady McTaratan? There's bound to be one who will make the main speech. If it is not to be Sir Alastair, who then?

Today Rory McTavish and his class are engaged in removing all surplus from the two classrooms to be used. This consists of heavy wooden blackboards on squeaky castors, tables and school desks, and these are put into the corridor in preparation for tomorrow's Prize-giving. This kind of school work is more to the liking of many of Rory's class than the usual. It means a complete uprooting of their traditionally dreary day, besides giving valid excuse for clattering and banging and all manner of noises uncondemned.

Ailie Chapman sits in the staffroom while her class disports itself in the playground to allow their domain to become one with Rory's. The platform in Rory's room has been moved to join the existing platform in Ailie's room, and the two have not made too happy a marriage, as they are not exactly a well-matched pair. Two boys are engaged in the enthralling task of testing for strength. This, to them, means bouncing up and down on it to make sure it will eventually stand the strain of the combined weight of the guests.

I have looked in to find out about the exact disposal of my Infant classes and find that, once they are dove-tailed together, the selected prize-winners condemned to the three front rows will be almost hanging onto the edge of the platform by their chins. I point this out to Rory, and after much jostling, a further three inches of space is achieved at the front. I leave him to worry how the prize-winners are to get out to receive their prizes and back again.

The platform extends along the front wall of the classroom and now reaches nearly to the door. Boys are bringing in chairs for the guests and setting them out in a long row at the back of the platform. I wonder who will have each chair, and I think that whoever is at the extreme end might find a chair leg hovering in space.

I find Rory and ask him about the Head's selection for the speech. Is it, I ask, to be Sir Alastair?

'Oh no,' says Rory. 'The Head has had a much better idea.'

'What's that?'

'It's to be a well-known Boy Scout – head of the County Scout movement, you know.'

'No, I didn't know. Won't he be rather young?'

'Oh no. He's a man over fifty. Been organizing for years. Great field worker, I believe.'

'Will he be dressed like a Scout?'

'Oh, sure. Goes about in it all the time. Fergus thought the children would be really interested in having someone like that rather than – oh, you know, the usual Chief Constable or something like that.'

'I certainly wouldn't think the Puddicks or the Gillogaleys would take to a Chief Constable.'

'He'll be wearing his medals and all that. I think he should make a hit. I must go now and see if the platform is steady enough for tomorrow.'

'Yes, of course,' I say. 'Be prepared.'

Before we leave the school today, Fergus Ogg informs us all about our places for the Prize-giving. He thinks the whole school can now be accommodated in the combined rooms.

'At a pinch,' he says, 'some can stand round by the side walls.' At a pinch!

My two assistants, Shirley and Marjorie, will be in control of all the Infant classes near the front. The piano will be over beside the window. The other teachers, including Rory, who will keep order at the back, will position themselves among their classes as strategically as possible. There will be two additional guests – the Boy Scout and Lady McTaratan's daughter, Cecilia, who will also be on the platform. This may make it rather a tight fit, but he hopes all the chairs will be accommodated, even at the ends. After arranging for the food to be sent to me early tomorrow, so that we can have it set out in time, he says that he hopes I am remembering that I shall be one of the platform party.

Who would forget that?

He follows this up by saying that the place allotted to me is on the chair at the farthest end of the platform nearest the door.

'In an emergency,' he says, 'quite easy for you to get off.'

Prize-giving Day

We are all early today and in our finery. Ailie is finishing her flower arranging, and carries the vases along to put on the tables.

'Thank goodness,' Daphne is saying, 'that we aren't having a concert this year. If there's anything I detest, it's having to put on a concert at a Prize-giving.'

'I agree,' says Rena. 'We had one two years ago. The last Headmaster made us produce the whole works – choirs, solos, oh, and those plays!'

'I was the wardrobe mistress,' says Daphne.

'And what was the Wardrobe?' I ask.

'Oh – pixie hats – Robin Hood tunics – fairy wings. What's more, I've still got them. Nobody knew what to do with them afterwards.'

'We had to make all the props ourselves, too,' says Rena.

'I'm going to get rid of them all soon,' says Daphne. 'They're stuffed in a box in the cupboard in my classroom, and I've hardly got space for the jotters.'

'They were made of all sorts of cloth,' says Rita. 'The mothers gave us old coat linings and bits of curtain. Cloth was hard to get then.'

'The Infant costumes were the only really bright ones. Somebody fished out some bright green and red sateen for pants. Very popular these were,' says Rena.

'I must speak to Barney about putting them all out before we go off for the holidays,' says Daphne. 'Absolutely useless now.'

'I wonder,' says Shirley, 'if Fergus will be wearing his kilt today, especially when we're having the landed gentry on the platform – and some wearing decorations, too, I'm told.'

'I'm afraid that I don't think I should really be on the platform,' I say, panicking at the last minute. 'Suppose something happens?'

'The Infants always used to have their own separate Prize-giving,' says Ailie. 'Having them along with the rest has never been done before.'

'The Head thinks they should be integrated with the rest of the school,' I say.

'They'll be so integrated,' says Vera, 'that we'll have to pull them apart to get them out for their prizes.'

To Shirley and Marjorie I say, 'Place yourselves near the door, just in case of anything unforeseen.'

'Near the door is where I'm to be,' says Daphne. 'You should be down among them,' she says to me, 'instead of up there.'

'I'll look to you, then,' I say sweetly.

'What good can you do up there anyway?' she adds.

'I can help to balance the weight so that the platform doesn't tilt,' I say. 'Also, I can see better who's fidgeting.'

'Let's hope,' she says, 'that the speech doesn't go on till Doomsday.'

Rory McTavish comes along to fetch me to go to the Head's room and meet the guests who have now arrived. The rest of the Staff are to supervise the placing of their classes, which was all rehearsed yesterday.

'We'll leave just as Lady McTaratan reaches the Dux Prize,' say Ailie and Vera, 'and slip along and make the tea.'

'Fine!' says Rory. And we both go along to the Head's room. The room seems filled to capacity already. I distinguish Fergus Ogg among the crush – and he is wearing an academic gown! Before I can decide whether this is preferable to a kilt, he introduces me to Sir Alastair and Lady McTaratan. Their daughter Cecilia is a stunner and no mistake. I wonder what Daphne's comments will be about this tall, fair-haired, immaculately groomed young woman.

Sir Alastair is a burly man, nearly as tall and muscular as Fergus and the virile Rory, but the man who is now next to be introduced to me, the distinguished 'boy' Scout, in the decorated style, is by contrast an insignificant man, moving at the level of the other men's middle jacket-buttons. He is clad in pale khaki shorts and his tiny knees seem immodestly bare. In his right hand he carries a large Baden Powell hat. I am confused by the sudden presentation to me of his left hand by way of greeting. Scout handshake, of course – as I suddenly realize.

I hastily change my handbag from my left to my right hand in order to meet left with left. It is so awkward that I drop my (presentation) handbag. The contents, including a small box of loose face-powder, spread themselves over Fergus Ogg's strip of luxurious drugget. Everybody dives down to retrieve my possessions, added to now by all the coins rolling out of my purse. In the mêlée I come into close quarters with the Boy Scout's bare knees and get smothered by the wings of Fergus Ogg's gown.

It is a somewhat dishevelled platform party that dusts itself down. To the tune of my apologies (which ought to have come from the Scout) we all go in procession to the room where the assembled school are restless with vociferous impatience, only partially controlled by a depleted Staff. The platform creaks as each of us steps onto it. I look at the leg of my chair poised a mere two inches from the outside edge. I gingerly lower myself onto the chair. And by this time there is an expectant, heavily-charged silence.

Rita strikes up *All Things Bright and Beautiful* and we all rise to sing, I with one foot clawed round the chair leg to keep it on the platform, which creaks again as we sit down.

The Minister says a prayer and it is just coming to an end when I catch sight of Edward McCartney (the closing of eyes is just not possible for teachers during prayers) performing his peculiar rite of 'tinkling'. Daphne is sitting quite near him in her place near the door. I signal violently to her, making strenuous mouths to indicate where the crisis has occurred. She suddenly sees me, and looks at the puddle slowly forming under Edward's chair. As it is coming relentlessly towards her beautiful suede shoes, she quickly grabs him and edges him out into the corridor.

The Minister extends his intercessions for the sins of the flesh by adding on the 'Lord's Prayer', in which everybody joins at breakneck speed. (There will be complaints about this afterwards, I'm sure.)

Fergus Ogg has remained unperturbed throughout, but rises magnificently when the Minister sits down. He gathers his gown round him like a toga, then gives it a good pull at both sides of the neck, and embarks on his school report. This is mercifully short, and he seems, more than anything else, keen to proceed to talking about his guests. He introduces them one by one and promises the children that they will eventually receive their prizes from the hand of the charming Lady McTaratan. Meanwhile, how would they like to hear from a real Boy Scout? Isn't that just the thing for the day the holidays begin? And won't some of them be going to Scout Camp? So —

The Scout rises. Well, hardly that, as, when he stands up, his head and shoulders are not much above the top of the table, the more so since the level of the Headmaster was of such elevation that I can almost see the eyes all jerking downward. Some of the Qualifying Class at the back of the room try to climb onto the row of desks they are sitting on. Rory McTavish makes threatening gestures at them.

'You will, I am sure,' the Scout is saying, 'all be anxious to begin your holidays — '

So far a first degree platitude. The children have been summing him up, trying to account for his size. He looks like the chap who helps the Scout Master with the Cubs, except for the medals and the heavy masculine voice. He drones on, and I catch a few phrases from time to time, my mind being now puzzled as to why Daphne has not returned. I am anxious, because Edward McCartney is a prize-winner and a very highly-strung boy. I will the Scout to go on a bit longer. Meanwhile —

'When I was in school,' he is saying (strange how many speakers eventually reach this point at Prize-givings), 'when I was in school,' he repeats, 'I was always careful to dot my tees and cross my eyes – '

Here he makes a significant pause. It is hushed and horrid.

'I was always,' he says again, 'careful to dot my tees and cross my eyes.' Here he giggles, but the response to the witticism is unforthcoming. But stay! a hand is indeed waving from among the prize-winners in the front row. The hand belongs to Augustus Ponsonby. The Scout sees it.

'Ah! Somebody wants to say something.' He looks at Augustus. I am hopeful it will not be a request to follow in the footsteps of Edward McCartney.

'Yes, little boy,' the Scout says encouragingly. 'Don't be afraid. Speak up.'

'Please, sir,' says Augustus in his clear incisive voice. 'It's dot your eyes and cross your tees.'

'Ha! H'm! Of course it is! – I wondered who would be quick enough to see that. Very good. Are you a Scout?'

'No, sir. I'll have to grow a lot bigger to be a Scout.'

I feel my ears grow hot, I do not know whether for Augustus or the Scout. He has rallied, however, and is finishing his speech.

– 'And when you all leave school and no longer have your teachers to depend on – then,' he says, 'if you belong to the Scouts, you will always have an anchor to fall back on!'

I could have thought of falling back on something more comfortable than an anchor!

The Scout can hardly be seen sitting down, I am sure. What this lowering must look like from the stalls I do not know, as my attention is now diverted to the outline of figures through the glass door. As the dutiful applause for the Scout is in progress, I feel sure the outline I see is Daphne's.

Fergus Ogg rises again and invites Lady McTaratan into her position for graciously presenting the prizes. Fergus begins at Primary One and is calling out the names. As my old class is now Primary Two A, there is still a minute or two for Daphne to bring in Edward, dry enough to receive his prize. Lady Mc-Taratan has now presented the two bashful beginners with their books and leans down to whisper a word in their ears as the applause breaks forth.

As Augustus (First Prize) sits down with his book, the door opens and a strange figure enters, followed by Daphne. She is propelling towards the platform what looks like a cross between a pixie and Robin Hood, just as Edward's name is called out. Some of the children begin to laugh, some look shocked, and the Qualifying are delighted and begin to cheer and stand again on the desks to see better. Rory McTavish pulls them down and hisses at those not near enough to manhandle.

Edward receives his second prize clad in a costume more properly adapted to a toadstool in Sherwood Forest. He wears a pair of knee-length red sateen pants, topped off by a bright green tunic with ragged edges, and takes his picture book in a kind of daze from Lady McTaratan, who never turns one single hair of her perfect perm under the fashionable hat. Daphne's face is nearly the colour of Edward's pants. Edward sits down to resounding cheers.

After the entire school has 'skailed' on a wave of further cheering, at this point only on behalf of the holidays, the debilitated Staff go along to Room Five to revive their morale with Fergus Ogg's food of the gods. Everybody is standing round with cups of tea and sandwiches in hand. There seem to be two separate camps at this stage, the guests and the Staff. I go over to the Staff nucleus.

'For Heaven's sake!' Daphne is saying, 'what else do you think I could have done?'

'The Boss will long remember his first Prize-giving in this school,' Rita says.

'One for his memoirs,' says Marjorie.

I say to Daphne, 'You saved the situation. I should have been blamed by Edward's father if he had missed getting his prize from the hand of Lady McTaratan. I take it you dipped into the props box you mentioned.'

Daphne is not wholly mollified. 'You should have been prepared for such a thing with your infants. Those who have been married know all these things.'

I stand reproved, venison pâté in hand.

'It was very resourceful of you,' says Ailie, already half-way through her third chicken vol-au-vent. 'As you say, it should never have happened.'

'Oh, rot!' says Shirley, 'it can and will happen, for ever and ever, you may be sure.'

'You see, he had to have the whole suit,' says Daphne, beginning to feel a bit of a heroine, 'he was more than merely – eh – wet, you see. I had a job cleaning him up. Of course, when you've had children in the house, you know all about it.'

None of her step-children, Vera once told me, were younger than fifteen years of age when she inherited them.

'Certainly,' says Rena, 'I'm not married, and I should never have known how to return him clean, dry and empty disguised as Robin Hood!'

'Oh, forget it,' says Vera, coming up with a plate of pheasant savouries, followed by Rita with a plate of cakes engulfed in whipped cream. 'Forget it, and taste what a real cake is like after these years of synthetics.'

Fergus Ogg is now steering the guests, including the elderly Scout, in our direction. We talk through the feast, and try to shake hands as they begin to depart as gracefully as possible after the morning of stress. The Scout shoots out his hand to Daphne. In great glee I watch as she tries to manipulate a handshake with her right hand, the left still holding a half-demolished wedge of cream sponge. The thumbs do not fit together and she ends by shaking a bunch of his fingers.

When by our combined efforts the last of the sumptuous feast has been absorbed and the dishes stowed away, we wish one another a happy holiday and begin to leave one by one. Some are for Continental holidays, the travel allowance having been increased.

Rena and Rita are off to the Austrian Tyrol, Vera to Holland, and Daphne, portentously maybe, only to Skye.

It is perhaps as well that she has already gone and misses the view I have, as I cross the deserted playground, of Marjorie stepping into Fergus Ogg's car.

I wonder, not about Marjorie or Daphne's private eye, as I go down the road, but about what mistakes are left for me to make next year.

August
1951

'I call it a scandal!'

Daphne's comment floats along the corridor to me as she leaves the staffroom. Regretfully, I have missed the succulent prelude to it, for this first morning of term I hurry directly into the room of enrolment and as hurriedly settle into the seat of acceptance. Outside, the now conditioned band of mothers stands in the Fergus-style queue and settles into a gabble of gossip.

Surprisingly, I am through the enrolment by the interval this time, only twenty-five having put in an appearance. This time also, birth certificates are automatically produced as if they were tickets at a turnstile, and every parent seems bent on packing her offspring into the classroom as if it were a railway compartment, and waving goodbye from the door.

The only temporary hold-up is with a Mrs McCracken, who insists her boy is called 'Gooey', although his birth certificate says 'Guy'. The boy himself is inhibited from speech by a piece of toffee which his jaws do not seem strong enough to pull apart. For the moment I am inclined to agree with his mother about 'Gooey'.

'I got his name out of one of these nice women's papers,' she explains, 'when I was lying-in, you know. The Minister's wife brought me a pile of lovely magazines when she came to see me. Such lovely names were in all the stories. I got Jilbert's and Sigh-ril's out of them as well.'

It is fortunate that the enrolment is completed early, as so far Marjorie has not turned up for duty. Shirley has taken her class along with her own, and unless Marjorie arrives later, will have to continue to do so until the afternoon.

I finish my list and when the rest of the school vacates the playground after the interval, I turn out my beginners to disport themselves for a few minutes. I am snatching a belated cup of coffee and hoping that when I go out to collect them again, none of them will have thought better of it and decided to go home.

Fergus comes along to see how it all went.

'Not so many this year,' he says.

'Only twenty-five so far,' I say. 'But there's tomorrow. How many should there be?'

'Twenty-seven in all, I believe,' he says. 'By the way, I went into your classroom before I discovered you were here in the staffroom, and I see you have been presented with a – token of esteem, or maybe it's the spoils of the chase – '

'Token of esteem?'

'Take a look. It's an unusual beginner. Let me have the completed list of entrants later today,' he says. 'Whether or not you add the latest one's name.'

Mystified, I hurry back to the classroom and take the recommended look – at a large and imposing cock pheasant standing on my desk. Stuffed, of course!

I examine it. Every feather is in place, and its feet are set in a compound of heather and moss glued to a wooden base. But it has a supercilious eye. I fail completely to guess Who, and go out to the playground to gather in the class. I count them all more than once and there are twenty-five. We go in and immediately a rush is made towards the pheasant, a horde of hands reaching and stretching to stroke its head, its wings, its tail.

'It's a nice peacock. I like it,' says Gooey.

'Not peacock,' I say. 'Pheasant.'

'I got a present for my birthday,' he says. 'It wasn't a bird. It was a penguin.'

Strive as I might, it is impossible to explain all the mistakes here and now.

'It's a pheasant,' I emphasize.

'Is the present for us?' asks another infant, name as yet not familiar to me.

'It seems to be,' I say.

'Who brought it?' asks another.

Finally, I have them all settled and investigating the new coloured felt designing sets, as being a tranquillizing medium. In the ensuing peace, I try to do some designing of my own, and fit the new names to the faces.

I come upon a discrepancy. I have enrolled no Bobby Burke, yet there is one who insists he is Bobby Burke. There should, on the other hand, be one called Michael Rourke, yet no one answers to this name.

'Which of you is Michael Rourke?' I ask.

'He's away home,' says a voice.

I approach the voice, which belongs to a solid-looking bullet-headed boy with a dour expression, who answers to Campbell McDermid.

'Well, Campbell,' I say. 'You seem to know Michael, and you say he went home. Did he not know it was only playtime and not dinner-time?'

'Oh, aye – he kent.'

'Then why did he go home?'

'Said he didna like the school much.'

I recoil from this unflattering comment. I had hoped it would have been merely confusion of timing. Half an hour on your first day at school must, I suppose, seem like a ten-year stretch to a five-year-old.

Now for Bobby Burke.

I question him and discover he is one of the tinker family returned from their roamings earlier this year, in time for Bobby to start school. He says his sister Jeanie brought him along and just left him in the playground along with the others.

'Your sister should have come to see me,' I say. 'In fact, your mother should have come.'

'She's got a baby,' says Bobby. 'She sent Jeanie.'

'I see, and where did Jeanie go after that?'

'Tae her class, after she did what me Mammy tell't her.'

'What was that?'

'She said to gie ye the bird.'

'The pheasant?'

'Aye. It's for a present.'

I can see I shall be committed to beginning a nature table, which is becoming all the rage in schools throughout the land these days. Certainly we are near enough to the moor up here to hear an occasional grouse or peewit. This year already we have found toads in the toilets, bees in the old belfry, and at present plenty of wasps on the windows. It will not be merely a nature table, but an incipient zoo.

Meanwhile, I thank Bobby as gracefully as I can, and wonder whether the pheasant is home-stuffed or a bargain from a Puddick-style jumble sale. I give one of the handsome feathers a tentative pull. It holds firm. Daphne has a predilection for fancy hats, so maybe I should keep the pheasant-present a secret just now.

Marjorie returns this morning. 'Temporary indisposition,' she says pedantically.

'Which being psychologically interpreted,' says Vera, 'means plain disgust at the thought of coming back.'

'Where did you go for your holidays?' Ailie asks her.

'A week in Skye and then a week in Harris,' says Marjorie.

'Popular place Skye,' says Vera. 'What with our Boss being there – and Daphne, of course, the last with Sherlock intentions.'

'I didn't see Daphne there,' says Marjorie. 'I avoid all teachers on holiday anyway.'

'You sound like Daphne her very self,' says Vera.

'Daphne had some very disturbing news about Skye yesterday,' says Ailie.

'Oh, Daphne likes to think she's disturbing,' says Vera. 'I wasn't in here yesterday at your gossip session. But I suppose Daphne was bursting with whatever it was. Anyway, what was it?'

'I'd rather not say,' says Ailie. 'Only Rita and Rena were here when she said it. You'd better ask her yourself.'

'Sounds promising,' says Shirley.

At that moment Daphne comes in. She has a new ensemble, in accordance with an unstated convention that you do not return after the holidays wearing the same rags you wore last session. Daphne's mood this time is pastel. She wears a pastel-blue coat over a pastel-pink dress, and a pastel-pink hat over a petunia make-up. She is still loyal to her old lipstick and cyclamen powder. The whole effect is cloudy-cherubic, the more so when, palely loitering at the pegs, she removes her hat and a pale cherubic perm emerges from the pink hat.

'Going somewhere special?' asks Vera. 'After school, I suppose.'

'Oh, well, partly,' says Daphne. 'Just a whist drive at the Women's Guild for Church Funds. I'm taking the place of the Provost's wife. She's off colour.'

Daphne isn't.

'Is the Provost going?' asks Vera.

'Oh, probably,' she says, somewhat too off-hand, I think.

'Ah, well, I suppose it brightens up your life,' says Vera.

'Oh, my life hardly needs brightening up,' she says. 'You've a different outlook when you're married, of course.'

'I didn't hear how you got on in Skye during the holidays,' goes on Vera.

'Surely you heard?'

'Heard what?'

'My news.'

'When a woman says that,' says Vera. 'She means, "look at my left hand".'

Daphne simpers and waves both hands, where she wears a wedding ring on each.

'Not yet for that,' she says, the more to stimulate our curiosity. 'No – my news is about another teacher, and one not far from here.'

'Sounds as if you had been at Delphi instead of Skye,' says Vera.

'Where's that?' says Daphne, caught again in Vera's trap.

'The news,' she goes on, 'concerns our Headmaster.'

'What has he been up to now?' says Marjorie.

'I heard – and in fact, actually saw – one or two things when I was in Skye.'

'Such as peat-hags and the jagged Cuillin?' says Vera.

'No. It was when I was in Portree, staying at the hotel.'

'Fishin' and shootin' and stalkin'?' says Vera. 'Were you stalkin' the Headmaster?'

'Of course not,' says Daphne, who takes umbrage under fire, 'but I heard disturbing rumours about him.'

'Why worry if they're only rumours,' says Vera.

'They were more than rumours,' says Daphne. 'Tangible evidence.'

'Of what?'

'Our outwardly correct Headmaster keeps an – establishment!'

'*Establishment*?' we all say at once.

'Really!' says Vera, 'we're far too long in getting to the point of all this. Who's supposed to occupy this "establishment"?'

'His children!' says Daphne. 'At least seven – or eight!'

'He must be married after all,' says Shirley.

'He's not!' says Daphne. 'That's the point.'

'A stag from the Cuillin,' says Vera.

'Rutting operation,' says Shirley.

'You are all very coarse,' says Ailie. 'I am greatly disturbed to think that all this is true, for I must say I have always had the highest regard for our Headmaster. It grieves me greatly to hear all this.'

'Perhaps before you let grief take over,' says Shirley, 'Daphne would tell us the evidence she says she has.'

'I was in the grocer's shop in the village one day,' she says, 'talking to the wife of the man who keeps the shop, and I happened to mention I was a teacher in the same school as a man from Skye.'

'Very subtle,' says Vera.

'If you want to hear, don't make any more comments,' says Daphne testily. 'The grocer lady asked his name, of course. She knew at once who it was. She said he was very popular on the island and fills his house with guests every summer.'

'Could be they were the guests' children?'

'Oh, no. She said the children came after the guests departed. Came from his establishment on the mainland, she said. Those are her very words.'

'What next?'

'A lot of trippers came in just then. When I went back next day she said he was very fond of children – and of the ladies, too.'

'Maybe when she said "establishment" she was just trying to translate a perfectly ordinary word from the Gaelic. The people there sometimes think in the Gaelic most of the year,' says Ailie, 'and get their English a bit rusty in the summer. Maybe she just meant a house.' Ailie's face begins to clear.

'I think that's just what it was,' says Shirley. 'It's all been a case of *honi soit* on your part, Daphne.'

'What's that?' asks Daphne.

Vera laughs outright. She is always delighted when Daphne reveals a gap in her knowledge.

'I agree, that's just it,' says Marjorie.

'Did you ask the shopkeeper why he wasn't married?' asks Shirley.

'Oh, yes, and she said something about a young man sowing wild oats.'

'Except that I shouldn't call Fergus young,' says Shirley.

'Certainly to you he must look quite old,' says Ailie, 'but to me he's a bit young to be a Headmaster. In my young days all the Headmasters had beards and were in their sixties.'

'There must be a good reason for him to keep all that kind of thing dark,' says Daphne, 'and what better place than Skye?'

'I vote we ignore this evidence,' says Vera.

'It's just your imagination, Daphne,' says Marjorie.

'And when I tell you that later I actually saw the kids, what will you say to that?'

'Saw them?' says Ailie.

'I did. The Post Office lady pointed them out to me the next day when she heard I came from a school near Greeninch.'

'And what actually took place then?' I ask.

'There was a utility van at the other end of the street,' Daphne goes on, 'and the postmistress pointed through the Post Office window and said, "Look! There are the kids from the big house." I looked out of the window and they were all getting into the van. They were too far away to see their faces very well.'

'Were you expecting to see a set of coffee-coloured piccaninnies, eh?' says Vera. 'Now, that would be something!'

'They seemed to be all ages. Unfortunately, I was rather late in finding out all this. We were leaving next day.'

'Pity you didn't manage to find out who his mistress was,' says Vera, 'after her supplying all that stock-in-trade for teachers. Seems there's a post-war bulge in Skye as well.'

'Don't be vulgar, Vera,' says Ailie.

'As a matter of fact,' goes on Daphne relentlessly, 'the postmistress, a nice lady with a Highland accent, said he seemed to be friendly with a "Mistress McLeod" somewhere near Applecross way. He sends quite a lot of letters there. And this lady was definitely installed in his house on the mainland. She emphasized the word "Mistress" too, when she said it.'

'Oh, tommyrot!' says Vera. 'That's the way some Scots still use the word instead of the more usual "Missis". The conclusion of your case for the prosecution wouldn't lead a jury to convict.'

'It's the most fantastic fabrication I ever heard,' says Marjorie. 'I can assure you it's far from the truth.'

And Marjorie marches out, looking exasperated.

'She must be in the way of knowing something, then,' says Daphne. 'I thought as much. But you can't keep secrets from a school Staff.'

And that, as far as I can judge, is the only credible statement Daphne has made today.

Marjorie is very late again this morning.

'Not quite got over it yet,' she says as she receives her class from Shirley.

My intention had been to let Shirley teach the enrolment class this term but until they are all finally enrolled and Marjorie is restored to punctuality, I have to take them myself. Three more arrive this morning, none of whom I can deflect to Homeston Primary. The roll to date is twenty-eight.

All the galleries are now gone from all the infant classrooms, and individual desks and chairs have been supplied. Marjorie and Shirley are delighted.

'The new Director of Education seems to be encouraging new ideas,' says Marjorie. 'I have heard that Fergus Ogg is a great friend of his. Maybe we'll get other priority improvements soon.'

'What other improvements?' I ask. I myself have not yet recovered from the shock of seeing all the new desks.

'For one thing,' says Marjorie, 'a light over my blackboard.'

'And for my room,' says Shirley, 'a new blackboard. No use a light just to show up a battered old score-board like mine.'

I look round their rooms, to show I am not out of touch with further modernization, ostentatiously making a note of all this in my diary. I go round and lift up the lids of the new desks.

'You had better see that the children don't leave anything in these desks,' I say. 'I mean food – their morning rolls or their fish suppers!'

'It's easy to clean crumbs out,' says Shirley. 'Look! Every desk has a hole punched in the bottom. All you need do is sweep the crumbs through.'

'Are you sure that's what the holes are for?' I say sceptically and with some sarcasm.

'Oh, yes, one of my friends in Homeston Primary has the same type of desk.'

'My new desks don't have them,' I say. 'And it's not a very large hole anyway.'

'This is a more advanced design,' she says, and I am already hopelessly out of date.

'I suppose,' I say, 'you have received your consignment of extra tools this term.'

'Oh, yes, a whole lot of hammers came with the heavy wooden builders. Sort of pile-driving stuff.'

'Then,' I say, 'the use of more than two of these at any one time is here and now proscribed – while I am next door.'

'Really?'

'Yes – really. And I recommend that you order sets of felt shapes for universal use next time you requisition – to balance the effect of a building site, you know.'

And feeling that I am perhaps reverting to type, but have shown who's boss, I return to my class to start the conditioning process.

Everything comes at once.

Besides new desks and chairs, we have new lavatories and wash-basins, and an imposing array of new pegs in the cloakroom. It is still not weather for coats to appear, and the new pegs are decorated at present with cleaners' feather dusters, brushes and even an odd pail or two.

I decide to begin instruction with regard to the new lavatories and, of course, the toilet rolls. These are in a big carton for which no home has yet been found, and this carton is under the new wash-basins. Rather spoils the desired effect. Armed with one of the rolls, today I march the class up to the new toilets with a view to showing them how to keep them always as new toilets. They all must learn how to deal with their own buttons, bows and braces. We march back again to the cloakroom where the toilet roll is installed on a ledge (newly constructed) with the same ceremony as a wreath on the Cenotaph. Solemnly we enter the classroom and I talk about getting names fixed to every article of clothing.

Since the day I was myself first installed, no day has ever gone so well.

September

Innovations seem to be budding off one from another like sea anemones. The district of Heatherbrae has acquired a bus of its own during the holidays. We can thus go down into the town at lunch-time if we so desire, and have a meal in *Nancy's Neuk*, a restaurant not far from the bus terminus. The days of sandwiches toasted on a fork at the staffroom fire have been superseded by a three-course meal in this new 'howff' with its checked gingham table-cloths. It has six tables in a sort of back parlour which has recently grown out like a bustle behind a sweetie-shop on Riverside Street.

The single-decker bus scuttles back and forth like a green beetle three times in the hour between Heatherbrae terminus and Riverside Street. It is already called 'The Wee Bus' in a town which has affectionate names for everything, animate or inanimate. If the same driver and conductress do not appear on it without fail every day, it is a matter of concern to the clientèle.

Sandy McLaren, the driver, is an ex-Service man. Desert Rat, he calls himself, although he has become a sleek one in the five years since he was demobilized. He is a substantial man with muscular hands and his cap is always at a slight angle from convention. His principal aim is the catching of schoolboys who run after his bus, which he brings to a shrieking stop the moment he 'feels' there is a body attaching itself to the rear.

The days of the attachment to the old sugar lorries have disappeared with the last war, and the bus provides a substitute – like saccharine for sugar, and certainly less satisfactory, for now you only get the ride and no delectable fistful of forbidden sweets. Sandy seldom catches any of these vampire bats, but he has sworn grim vengeance when he does. Towards this purpose he keeps a notebook. Today he asks me for the name of our Headmaster. Not for hanging onto lorries, or buses, but because he intends to visit our school some day, and have a word with him. Aye, and with the Head of St Bride's as well, where a whole swarm come onto the bus, legitimately right enough, every day, but who provide cover for the rascals that travel 'by their wits', as Sandy says. I tell Sandy that I am doubtful if their wits are good enough to take them very far.

The conductress, Bridie, is a thin little spinster, much more like a desert rat than Sandy, and even sharper. She says she used to be a land-girl. She loudly asserts that she has no use for men, who, she insists, are much inferior to cattle and horses. The men passengers chaff her about her boy friends, especially about a bulky winking policeman who has taken to travelling regularly at lunch-time. Jokes about the attraction she appears to have for this constable always bring forth a slash of scorn.

'I wouldna hae him,' she says, 'if he were given away with a pound o' tea.'

After all the battling boys from St Bride's have emptied themselves off the bus, she says to me,

'I don't know how anybody could ever be a teacher, and try to put anything into the heids o' weans like them. Preserve me frae weans. I'd rather hae piglets ony day, and goats are a treat compared to them. What a life it must be in a school!'

'I don't think I could ever be a bus conductress,' I say, 'and work till six o'clock.'

'In the War I worked frae dawn till dusk at the farm. Buses are jammy to that. How many hae ye got this time?'

'Twenty-eight,' I say.

'Twenty-eight weans! Imagine that! – Ye'll be gettin' Sandy's wee laddie soon.'

'The enrolment's complete,' I say. 'He should have been at the school ten days ago.'

'Sandy's just flitted into the new hoose yesterday, so wee Sandy wasna eligible till today, as ye might say.'

Today Sandy the Second is enrolled, and for him and the other late arrivals, I have to begin the reading preliminaries all over again. I have now told the first of the pre-reading stories four times.

'We had that story yesterday,' says Bobby Burke. I patiently point out that Sandy has not had the privilege of hearing it before. Nor, I add to myself, has he had the lessons about what to do with buttons, bows and braces.

Sandy conforms to first-day pattern by failing to return to the classroom after the morning interval. I question the know-ledgeable Bobby Burke about it. Bobby has emerged as a Super-clipe of great dependability.

'He's still up in the toilet,' Bobby says.

'Why didn't you wait for him?'

'The bell rang,' says Bobby.

We proceeed with the lesson, and are all carried away by the production of some life-size pictures to match the stories. Temporarily I forget Sandy. I suddenly realize this, and go to the window which has a view of the toilet area at the top of the playground. No sign of Sandy. I decide to wait for a few more minutes and get the class settled to counting blocks and wooden shapes. Then I shall go out and see what is keeping Sandy. Braces, in all likelihood.

I take another glance out of the window.

Sandy is on his way down the playground. He is trailing a confusion of shoes, braces, shirt and pants along with him.

Sandy himself is as naked as a newt.

I dash out, run into the staffroom, snatch my jacket off the peg, fly out into the playground and envelop Sandy in the jacket. Just in time! Daphne emerges from the side entrance with her class. Her back is towards me for the second of time it takes me to hustle Sandy through the door. Maybe it's all right if you're married, of course!

It takes nearly a quarter of an hour before, in the privacy of the staffroom, I can disentangle the shirt, pants and braces from the puzzle-net they have become. Clothed and in his right mind, he comes back into the fold, mercifully not bleating.

I sit at the desk while I recover from the hazard of first days. I am no sooner seated than a demure girl comes in from Shirley and hands me a note. Shirley always chooses demure girls to deliver notes. This note says,

'There is a DOE coming up the playground.'

After what I have already seen coming along the playground nothing would surprise me. But I jump up and look out of the window. I can see nothing. Shirley has a window which looks onto the front playground, whereas mine are all to the back.

A doe?

Last week I had a swift down the fan-light, and a panicky sparrow in the corridor. I write at the bottom of the note: 'Where did it come from? Can't see it from this room.'

I give the note back to the demure girl. Soon it returns with the answer, 'It comes from the Education Offices. You were out the first time when I came to warn you.'

Shirley's messenger has no sooner gone than the door opens again and Fergus Ogg brings in a man I have never seen before. This man, at least, is not wearing his hat.

'Our Director of Education,' he says. 'Come to see how your infants are doing.'

The DOE!

DOE phobia has apparently replaced Inspector phobia, especially among probationers, who favour an early warning system.

The DOE walks round admiring all his administration has done for us. I assume a suitable expression of gratitude. Before they go Fergus says that it is likely we shall be introducing a system of 'streaming' next term. On this liquid note they depart for Marjorie's room, where now appropriately sits Edward McCartney.

The staffroom topic is, of course, the new Director of Education. As usual origins and peccadilloes are important to Daphne.

'Where is he from?' she asks.

'From Xanadu,' says Vera wickedly.

'Where's – ?' Daphne stops short, nearly off her guard.

'I mean,' Vera says, 'that he's from that over-heated pleasure dome up at Admin.'

'I know that,' says Daphne, 'what I mean is, where does he originate?'

Nobody knows this.

'I think,' ventures Shirley, 'it's from somewhere on the East coast. He's a graduate of St Andrews.'

'Is he married?' This, of course, from Daphne.

'As far as I know, he's engaged,' says Shirley.

'To a teacher?'

'No – to a research scientist, or something.'

'One of my sons is a research scientist,' boasts Daphne. 'Agriculture and Fisheries actually. But what I'd like to know is where you get all your information.'

'Got it from Marjorie.'

'Who, I expect,' says Daphne, 'got it from Fergus Ogg. Incidentally, I wonder why Marjorie is not in yet?'

Shirley takes over Marjorie's class – until ten o'clock she says, when she is due to go on to the Gym, which will only hold one class. I take the hint.

But Marjorie arrives at five to ten.

'Sorry,' she says, 'I don't seem to have got over my last bout – of infection. Was quite seedy again.'

Shirley departs Gymwards, Marjorie's door closes, and I pray for a boring, humdrum day.

It is only five minutes before Marjorie is in my room again with a look of extreme anxiety on her face. A request to go home? I fervently hope not.

'It's Charlie Chapman!' she bursts out. 'He's got his finger jammed in the hole inside his desk.'

Charlie Chapman! I might have known that, if anybody was destined to be a pioneer of the new hazard, it would be Charlie, the primary pest of Primary Two B.

I hasten in to Charlie – a distant relative of Ailie Chapman, but apparently not distant enough, since she has been apologizing for him ever since the first day he was sent to plague us. Charlie's unfortunate name has caused red-eared embarrassment to every teacher he has encountered. Invariably he is called out as 'Charlie Chaplin'. To bolster this notion, he is a comedian in his own right, much given to creating diversions, as well (according to Barney) as being a Limb (of Old Nick, he means).

I might have known that these holes in the desk would suggest a dramatic situation to Charlie. There was something about them that stirred in my sub-conscious the first day I saw them. From the beginning they held promise of prisoners, real or induced.

Charlie, with the lid of his desk propped up, sits with his arm stretched below it, and his forefinger weaving up through the hole like a questing snake.

'He says he can't pull it out,' says Marjorie, suppressed hysteria in her tone.

I decide that in my position I must undoubtedly show imperturbability, and take cool command in the most nerve-racking situation.

'Can't you possibly pull it out, Charlie?' I ask in a low conversational tone. 'Don't panic.' I say this more to myself than to Charlie. I also suspect that maybe Charlie is as much held prisoner by visions of fame as by his finger.

'No, miss,' he says.

'Try, Charlie.'

Charlie wiggles his finger. No result. I bend down and test for deceit. Sure enough, the finger will not pull out, even when I pull his hand from below.

'What on earth are we going to do?' Marjorie's voice wobbles into the upper register.

'We'll get some lubricant,' I say. 'Butter – or something.' Marjorie runs immediately into the staffroom, but returns empty-handed.

'Not a scrap of butter left in the cupboard,' she says, 'this was the day we were to buy in a new supply.' I go back to my room and fish out a tube of cold cream from my cosmetic case. Marjorie looks at me with hope and a kind of adoration as I proceed to anoint the finger as near to the jammed joint as I can work it in.

But no anointing does any good. Charlie's finger remains a toad-in-the-hole.

'Cold compresses!' I say, inspired. 'Shrink it, of course!'

We apply bits of cotton wool from the first-aid box soaked in cold water. I wrap it round the finger, and wait.

'Allow to stand,' I say lightly, to encourage Marjorie, 'until shrunk.'

Marjorie calms the excitement of the class, who look disappointed that nothing more dramatic than cold cream and compresses is going to happen to Charlie.

'Can you pull it out now?' I say, five minutes of frantic freezing having passed.

Charlie pulls, but no result. The class shiver with delight. What now?

Diane-Dora Ponsonby, now in the top section of the class, is looking contemplatively at the finger.

'Perhaps,' she says at last, 'Charlie will have to take his desk home with him tonight.'

'Not at all,' I say, 'we'll get it out, I'm sure.' But I'm not sure.

'If he took it home, his Daddy could saw the desk in two,' goes on Diane, 'then his finger could come out.'

'Or maybe,' suddenly puts in Walter Gardiner, 'his Daddy could saw off the finger.'

'Walter!' shouts Marjorie. 'Hold your silly tongue! You'll frighten Charlie.'

And indeed, Charlie by this time, now that the tension is rising into imponderables, is beginning to look a little as Marjorie looked this morning on her arrival at school.

'I think,' I say to her, 'you'd better go along and report this to Fer –' (not in front of the children!) 'Mr Ogg, before any further steps are taken. We've done all in our power.'

Marjorie goes rushing out of the class as quickly as any Gillogaley and, in no time at all, Fergus appears on the scene, Marjorie now looking greatly relieved. Fergus examines the finger, removing our cold compresses.

'We've done all we could,' I say.

'I can see that,' he agrees. 'Maybe we shall have to do something more drastic.'

'Oh – no!' says Marjorie, 'not –'

He drops his voice and says to us, 'There's luckily a joiner in the school today, working at those ill-fitting doors in the girls' toilets. Maybe he's got some tools – '

'Will he have to cut the desk?' I ask.

'Could be – ' says Fergus, 'I'll bring him along and we'll see what he suggests.'

I continue to apply cold compresses to Charlie's finger, which has now turned a pale petunia colour like Daphne's lipstick. There is a certain Charlie Chaplin pathos in the drama.

We wait.

The door opens again and Fergus Ogg comes in, brandishing a workmanlike brace-and-bit. He is accompanied by the joiner holding a big saw and a small saw.

Charlie takes one comprehensive look at them – and out comes the finger!

To whom, I wonder, are the honours due?

October
1951

It is Thursday, and the 'Wee Bus' is delayed at lunch-time. The wrathful Desert Rat, his teeth bared, stops it half-way to the school. He descends from his driver's seat with the rapidity of a squirrel, but the boy who has been attached to the back of the bus has already a fair lead along the path that goes into the well-wooded public park. All the passengers crane curiously forward to see what they can see of the chase, but the chaser and the chased have by now disappeared among the laurels. We sit and wait. It is coming on to half-past one, when I ought to be within the confines of the school. I am torn between the need to be in time and the need to see the culprit brought to justice. I hope that it will be one of St Bride's adventurers and not one of Heatherbrae's. Whenever it has been one of Heatherbrae's, the reproachful looks of the other passengers seem always to be directed at me rather than at the sinner.

It turns out to be one of Heatherbrae's. Sandy McLaren, triumph and vengeance blended in equal proportions on his face, marches the culprit back through the park gates by the collar of his jacket. Identification is still uncertain, but Sandy's voice is shouting behind the huge bonnet of the bus.

'On you get, you brat o' Hell, you! On! D'ye hear?' All we can hear in response is a wail in crescendo. Then the boy is pushed up the step onto the platform. The brat o' Hell is none other than Francis Gillogaley.

'Now,' says Sandy, banging the door shut, 'you sit up there at the back. D'ye hear? Up to the back wi' ye, double quick, and stay there!'

Francis is reluctant, so Sandy yanks him by the arm and deposits him bodily on the back seat.

'If it's a ride ye're wantin',' says Sandy, 'ye'll get it. I'll take ye for a ride, and ye'll no' be wantin' anither!'

'I'll be late for the school,' wails Francis. 'Please, I'll no' chase the bus again. Honest I'll no'. Let's oot noo – '

'Nae fear!' says Sandy. 'Ye're goin' to get yer fill o' rides. An' if ye're late for school, who's to blame for that, eh?'

'I'll get the strap, so I will,' bleats Francis.

'I was hoping ye would,' says Sandy. 'It's better than losin' yer life, and me getting blamed. In fact,' he goes on, 'the later ye are, the harder ye'll get lammed. So I'm taking you right to the terminus and back!'

Francis lifts his voice into high C and sobs loudly. Sandy goes back to the driver's seat and starts up the bus. I am sitting near the front.

'Will he get strapped?' he asks.

'Possibly,' I say. 'But don't relent. It'll teach him a lesson. He's been working up for this for a long time. Serves him right. Have a nice journey.'

And, heartless teacher that I am, I alight.

The bus passes up the road from the school on its way to the terminus. Out of the back window of the bus I see Francis looking longingly at the school for the first time in his life.

As I go up onto the front area there is not a child to be seen, and an unnatural hush pervades the empty playground. Usually there are crowds of children playing around or walking tentatively on the low coping which edges Barney's newly-planted daffodil garden.

It suddenly occurs to me that I must be very late. But not so late maybe as Francis will be. I look at my watch, which comfortingly says that I have three more minutes to make my entry before the bell is rung. Where, then, is the school population? Normally the front playground has a row of 'staked claims' in the form of school-bags and jackets thrown down to mark the place where the proud owner will be the leader in the lines when the bell rings. Today there is neither bag, boy nor girl.

I go in to a perfectly empty school, and can see nobody in any of the classrooms. But as I pass through this hollow shell, I seem to hear a distant roar, as if I were approaching a football ground on a Cup Final day. The noise grows louder as I get nearer the rear of the school. I open the door leading into the back playground and am almost felled by a Hampden roar coming from what seems to be the entire school all together in one place. The noise is rhythmical –

'Aah! Oh!' A pause.

'Ooh!' Another pause.

'Aw! Oh! – Hurray!'

Among the shouting mob is an inordinate number of balls. Balls are everywhere. I go out into the playground and a ball bats my hat over one eye. Balls are flying, rolling, bouncing. Faces are all looking up at the roof. I look up too. It is from here that the balls are coming. Barney is on the roof and keeps up a constant hail of balls from the gutters. The 'oo's' and the 'ah's' are the escapes of steam from the crowd at every new bullet. They cascade down as I watch – rubber balls, golf balls, tennis balls, sorbo bouncers, burst balls, coloured balls, half balls and even small footballs. Every ball that has been lost on the roof for a decade seems at last to be returning to base. Whoops of delight and snarls of possession accompany giddy chases all over the playground. Fights for possession are well advanced.

'It's mine!'

'It's no'. It's mine!'

'I lost it last September!'

'So did I!'

'I lost mine up there last summer. It was a sorbo!'

'It's no' yours. It's mine. Mine had a chip out o' it. Look! there's the mark. The dog bit it! So it's mine.'

'Old Gurney wouldna get mine down for me. But it was above the door, so it was. And that's it!'

And so it goes on.

Old Gurney had sworn he would dislodge no ball that was thrown up onto his roof, so the accumulation was one of years, like humus in a wood.

The bell rings. But not a child seems to hear it. The ball orgy goes merrily on. The Puddick family seems to be winning, the Gillogaleys being no more than one tennis ball behind. Balls are secreted in pockets, cradled in arms, stuffed up jerseys. Highwaymen continue to loot and claimants to protest.

Rory McTavish appears at the back door with the school bell in his hand. He supplements this with a whistle, upon which he blows three sharp blasts. The noise at last tails away, and, dripping balls from their persons, the children scatter to their various class lines where they form up like iron filings arranging themselves to the poles. For Fergus Ogg has appeared.

'What's going on?' he asks.

'Barney's clearing the gutters of all the lost balls.'

'Yes. The slaters are here. It's a pity he didn't wait until after the assembly. It's well over time already.'

'He says he's well over his lunch-time already too,' says Rory.

I go along later to Rory's class to tip him off about Francis and his penance. By this time Rory, with masterly organization, has every ill-gotten ball in a large box, to await legitimate claims, in writing, with description, date of loss – and signature. This afternoon's English exercise.

'I'll be very stern with Francis if he turns up,' he says. 'Was he impertinent to Sandy?'

'We-ll,' I say. 'Not exactly. But I'm sure Francis has died a thousand deaths already. Maybe we'll have a visit from his mother tomorrow.'

'Sandy had better look out, then,' says Rory. 'Maybe she'll refuse to wash his bus tonight.'

It is, however, Sandy himself who comes up to the school today, Friday, notebook in hand and pencil at the ready. He is in the queue outside Fergus Ogg's door along with the Attendance Officer and Mr Mullen, the Protestant partner of the Mixed Marriage.

Mr Mullen has a grim determined look on his face. He ignores me as I pass by, so I am fairly certain that I can have committed no transgression against the Mullen family, otherwise he would be springing out of the queue to pin me down.

But the vibrations from this queue have never been less harmonious.

For once I have steered through my morning's work with no interruptions bar the normal. But at half-past eleven Fergus Ogg comes in.

'The Mullens are leaving,' he says. 'Look out the Record Cards for those in the Infant Department and fill them up – to date of today.'

'Are they leaving the town?'

'Oh, no, just the school. The father is transferring them all to St Bride's as from Monday.'

'The whole six?'

'That's right. The lot.'

'What reason did he give for that?'

'The ostensible reason is that he believes they won't be harried in St Bride's the way they are in Heatherbrae.'

'Who's been harrying them?'

'Nobody, I'm sure. The real reason is sheer cussedness and to get his own back on his wife. He and his wife had one of their famous quarrels.'

'He might have given us more notice of the withdrawal. It's a lot of extra work – and at the last minute.'

166

'The row didn't take place till this morning.'

'I wish they'd resolve their differences one way or the other. Hasn't this been going on for years?'

'More or less. The children's education is just one of the bones of contention. It's always good for another row.'

'Dad, the Protestant, wants to show his authority over the household, and makes it a point of honour to differ from his wife, so he puts them in the Catholic school. It's the queerest set-up.'

'By the way, when you have time, I should like a list of any children you think belong to problem families.'

'I'll do that next week.'

'Oh – and are you conversant with Intelligence Testing?'

'Apart from the usual College surveys, I've never done any in the schools.'

'I'll let you have a look at some of the tests. Meanwhile, the Mullens' Cards, please.'

'I hope they're removed for good. That would be one of your problem families gone.'

The sudden removal of the Mullen family is today's topic. Ailie says that the two children in the upper classes have been kept off this afternoon. No one knows why, except that it's Friday. Nobody has a good word for the Mullens, whose Records Cards and Attendance Cards have to be made up at a time when everybody not only has a register to make up but also an Age List, which never fails to reduce every member of Staff to a palsied wreck whenever it is demanded. The staffroom is a sparking fireworks of imprecations and prophetic doom for the Mullens.

'I'll be here till five o'clock,' says Daphne. 'I've a mistake in my register and it's no wonder. I've been over it ten times and still I can't find it.'

'I'll look at it for you,' offers Ailie. 'Somebody else can usually spot it at once.'

Daphne melts into gratitude.

My two probationers are clamouring for help with the Age

Lists. It is a quarter to five when we all finally creep out of the school. Daphne by that time has found her mistake, or rather, Ailie has found it.

'She lost one of her tens,' she says.

Daphne blames the Mullens for making her late for the hairdresser. As she has almost lost her perm as well as her ten, her hair is standing up like a lot of exclamation marks, with the added loss of her temper. A shampoo is her only therapy.

'At least,' says Vera, 'we'll not have the Mullens to complicate life for us after today.'

Fergus Ogg and Rory McTavish are even later than we are. Rory is going through the registers like a ferret in a rabbit hole to catch any mistakes. Fergus is checking the Age Lists and this is a day where he more than earns his responsibility element. We pray that on Monday morning none of us will get the lists back to correct any errors.

What we get back on Monday is not, however, our errors – but the Mullens.

The first thing to greet the Head this morning is a queue of Mullens outside his door, headed by mother Mullen. She is very fashionably dressed, in high-heeled court shoes and a red coat. She wears no hat, which detracts somewhat from the urban sophistication of her ensemble. But this is by design, for her jet-black hair is drawn up into a high muffin on top of her head. It is held in this precarious position by an upstanding Spanish comb. Her eyelashes are mascara'd, and correspondingly charcoaled eyebrows must, I imagine, hypnotize Fergus into thinking he is entertaining Carmen.

After her audience with the Head (whose reactions I should have given a week of my holidays to see) she brings round the two youngest Mullens to restore them to their original niches. She has enrolled the whole family again in Heatherbrae as a counter-measure to Friday's extraction. The education in St Bride's is not what she would want for her children. Mr Mullen's capitulation has been effected over the week-end. I should have given another week of my holidays to have been able to listen-in to her method.

'Here they are back for ye,' she begins, assuming, of course, that I have been feeling deprived over the week-end.

'I thought,' I say, 'that Mr Mullen was determined they should be transferred to – '

'I'll fight for my children to the bitter end,' she breaks in, with the air of a female spider set on eating her mate. 'They've been fine in this school, but there's no holding him when he gets an idea into his head. He does it to spite me.'

'He did it to spite us too,' I cannot forbear saying. 'It gave us an unconscionable amount of work – all for no reason.'

'I can't see why taking them away gave you work. It would be less to teach.'

(This is one of the popular superstitions – that we are only teaching all the time.)

'I suppose the Headmaster told you we had all their forms to fill in. They must be sent off to Headquarters by this time. Maybe they'll not allow us to take them back.'

I cannot help this bit of hand-smacking. She richly deserves bottom-slapping as well. And she looks suitably apprehensive, much to my delight.

'The Master never said that to me.'

'Well, it's true. Surely your husband told you about all the Records and Transfer forms.'

'That he never did. Just let him wait till I get back. I'll be having something to say to him about that. Are ye going to keep them?' she adds anxiously.

'For the time being,' I say reluctantly. 'Maybe you'd better say no more to your husband. It might stir up further trouble.'

'Trouble! It's never me that causes the trouble. It's him. Ye know this, miss – that man'll drive me into my grave some day, that he will. I'll be driven to doing something to myself, miss!'

'Oh, nonsense!' I say. 'Think what that would mean to your children.'

'I've threatened it before. Some day I'll do it. That I will.'

I take the children in and restore them to their pedestals, and thankfully see the Spanish tragedy off the premises, still protesting about what she will do to herself. Right now, I feel like doing it for her.

Today we hear that Mrs Mullen has done something to herself. Vera brings the news.

'Mrs Mullen has done it!' she announces.

'Oh, dear!' says Ailie. 'That's terrible! A very unbalanced woman I've always said. Has she – did she – ?'

'She has,' says Vera. 'I just saw her just now down at the school gate!'

'But I thought you said she had done – something . . .'

'Ah!' says Vera. 'But what you mean is different from what I mean. What Mrs Mullen has done is typical of Mrs Mullen. She has changed herself overnight from a dark Spanish beauty into a dazzling Teutonic blonde!'

December

An unusual thing has been taking place over the last two months. We have been left in peace to teach! Whether this is due to Fergus Ogg having severely pruned the number of interruptions or whether it is merely a benevolent indifference on the part of fate, none can tell. And I have, in fact, actually had time to look over the promised Intelligence Tests, which seem even more like parlour games than they were at College. They have an air of high-class glossy comic strips. Maybe I am becoming imperceptibly old-fashioned, and should bring myself up-to-date, for I have an uneasy feeling that Fergus has something up his Harris tweed sleeve.

Barney's bulbs are already poking their sharp green noses out of the soil in the front garden of the school, which is reclaimed land, filched from the greensward. Primary Seven has been further deturfing sections of the remaining grass with intense horticultural zeal, in order to make more flower beds.

The bulbs we planted in September are coming up on the windowsill. No need to put them in a cool dark cellar in this school. We live in a cool dark cellar in this school most of the winter, the heating being no better than it was in the deep-freeze days in Garlock St. Fergus wants all the classes to compete in the Spring Bulb Show, which the little Provost with the lamp-post is enthusiastically sponsoring as a Corporation project.

Not only are the bulbs coming up, but Christmas is also coming up. With it comes an orgy of the arts, this time less of the plastic arts and more of the theatrical. No teacher is to attempt to coach the David Garricks or the Mrs Siddonses. It is to be a free-for-all in which no Staff dare meddle. Information leaks along the usual channels, that is, via the innocent infants. In all the families where the brothers and sisters are leading ladies (or gentlemen) they boast at the tea-table every night about how impressive their parts are. It seems that Cinderella is the theme. Under the tutelage of Douglas Ponsonby (a cousin of Augustus) Primary Seven are in the Gym every day at three o'clock, working themselves up to concert pitch as the last week before the holidays approaches.

It is all very professional. Douglas has appointed himself as Director, Martin McCartney (Edward's brother) as Producer, and Mary Farquharson as Wardrobe Mistress. He has thus effectively robbed his cast of the real brains of the class, and left himself with actors that cannot remember their lines. There is, however, no lack of fools rushing in for angels' parts, and this little matter of learning lines does not emerge while the haggling for the principals goes on.

The part of Cinderella is hotly contested. Douglas's choice finally settles on Jeanie Burke, she being able to obtain some convincing rags for her costume, or so she says, and this sways the committee in her favour. Lorna Chapman is appointed Fairy Godmother. Douglas discovers today the memorizing difficulty, especially among the male cast, so we hear he has appointed himself to the part of Prince as well. He puts out a call for the Two Ugly Sisters and the Stepmother. Francis Gillogaley and Jamsie Puddick rush to apply for the first and Michael Mullen for the second.

All seems well until we hear that Marigold Puddick has been fiercely contesting her right to Fiona's part of Fairy Godmother. Props are being supervised by Rory McTavish, but he dare not lay a hand on them, this all having to be 'their very own work', the edict having been issued by Fergus Ogg. A great deal of painting on pieces of canvas is being done, in the playground when the weather is bearable, and in the corridor when it is not. It is thus mainly done in the corridor, so that movement throughout the school is serpentine. Today this is particularly bad, as the playground at this moment would be better fitted to a production of *The Ice Maiden*.

Today we hear that Marigold Puddick has taken measures counter to *Cinderella*. Marigold has appointed herself Director of – another play!

Bunty tells me about it.

'My sister's in a play,' she says proudly.

'Has she got into *Cinderella* at last, then?'

'No. She couldna get into *Cinderella*. Douglas Ponsonby wouldna let her.'

'Oh? What's she doing now, eh?'

'*Away In a Manger*.'

'Oh, I see. She's singing carols instead. A good idea.'

'Oh, no, it's no' carols. It's a play. She made it up. The three wise men are in it.'

It transpires that Marigold, a thwarted Godmother, has retaliated by producing her own play. *Cinderella* is in serious difficulties, as Marigold has treacherously drawn off Francis Gillogaley, Jamsie Puddick, Michael Mullen and Jeanie Burke. Douglas Ponsonby is airy about it – relieved maybe.

'They couldn't say their lines anyway,' he says loftily. 'We'll make it up with the cleverest from Primary Six. They'll be far better.'

'Won't the defaulters let Marigold down too?' I say, when Douglas comes round with his programmes for the Show.

'Oh, no. Marigold's play is what you call a mime. Nobody needs to speak.' How resourceful of Marigold!

'What about the use of the Gym?' I ask.

'We'll still keep that. *Away In a Manger* is a kind of – travelling circus,' says the erudite Douglas contemptuously.

And that is indeed what it is. The strolling players visit you where you sit. No need to move into any Gym. No cumbersome scenery. No lines to learn.

Jamsie Puddick is the Donkey. Very well cast.

Francis Gillogaley is the First Wise Man. A sublimation?

The other Wise Men are Michael Mullen and Bambi Puddick. Jeanie Burke is Mary. The remaining Puddicks fill in the other parts. I have heard that Marigold has been going the rounds of the Homeston Council houses with the pram of nefarious memory in order to collect cast-offs for the costumes.

This week, the last of the term, we all go in turns to the Gym to see *Cinderella.* The Gym only holds one class for its legitimate purpose, but manages to hold two classes and a stage when turned into a theatre. The production is a great success, and we all agree we could have seen no better in the King's Theatre in Glasgow.

No lessons are possible between our attendances at the Heatherbrae Playhouse and the visits of the itinerant Miracle players of Marigold's entourage. It is both a miracle and a mystery how Marigold has succeeded in guaranteeing a perfect attendance at school for a whole week of the entire Puddick, Gillogaley and Mullen families. And there is no doubt about it that, while *Cinderella* has been a highly creditable performance, *Away In a Manger* has been the hit of the season.

The applause has been heard resounding to the belfry of Heatherbrae during the final days of the term, as encore performances are demanded by all the classes. This success must be attributed to the verisimilitude of Marigold's production, the whole appeal of which has been the use of a real cat, a puppy, a guinea pig, a budgie and two white mice for the animals in the stable. I for one was a little surprised that Marigold had not signed on a donkey, especially as the Burkes were an integral part of the production. I have heard that the white mice belong to

Augustus Ponsonby, and that there was a right royal row when Augustus offered them to the persuasive Marigold instead of to Douglas for use in *Cinderella*.

Besides the real animals, Jamsie Puddick's donkey's head, (made, we are told, by father Puddick) gives a hint of a *Midsummer Night's Dream*. Francis Gillogaley, attired heavily in towels, makes an impressive Wise Man. For the final performances Marigold goes a step further, and induces Jeanie Burke to bring along the latest Burke baby (now nearly a year old) to add to the Grande Finale.

Marigold has had other ideas about her play during the week. Its initial success having been assured, she comes round to all the classes and asks if the children will bring a penny for the encore performance.

'Have you asked Mr Ogg about that?'

'Oh, yes, miss.'

'Did he give you permission to make a charge?'

'Oh, yes, miss.'

'What do you intend to do with the money?'

'I'll gie it to Mr Ogg.'

'For the School Fund?'

'He says for me to think o' something I'd like to do with it.'

'Since you have permission, we'll ask the children if they'd like to bring something for the collection.' Marigold goes away delighted, but I have some misgivings – knowing Marigold.

This afternoon we are having an encore performance. I am sitting along with Shirley and Marjorie and their two classes all crammed in together in Marjorie's room. My own class has been dismissed at twelve-thirty today and I am attending the performance for the second time. Shirley is at the back of the room with her class, and Marjorie is directly behind me as the play proceeds. The Infant classes are entranced with the live animals, convulsed by Francis Gillogaley in his bath robes, and moved to worship by the rather oversize newly-born baby in a clothes basket.

'Can we take the collection now?' asks Marigold. She instructs the donkey to take round a leather helmet belonging to Jamsie, while the three Wise Men bring round the animals and the baby for the audience to get a closer look at them. Luckily the white mice are in a cage. Cries of 'Oh!' and 'Ah!' mingle with the sound of pennies dropping into the helmet.

'By the way, Marigold,' I say, 'have you decided yet what you're going to do with the money you collect?'

'Oh, aye,' she says. 'It's to go to help the dumb animals.' (Donkey and all?)

Jeanie Burke has difficulty preventing Baby Burke from being smothered both by the long white shawl in which she is arrayed for the play and by the attentions of Primaries Two AB.

As Jeanie finally reaches the front with the baby and prepares to depart on a final curtain with the rest of the players, Charlie Chapman pipes up, 'Please, miss, my Mammy's to get a new wee baby in the spring-time, so she is.'

'Now, isn't that nice!' I say, turning to Charlie. 'That'll be a big day for you.'

Just as I say this, I hear Marjorie's voice very close to my ear saying in a tense, super-charged whisper,

'And it'll be a big day for me as well. I'm having a baby in May. Do you think I could speak to you in private, please?'

Marjorie speaks to me later after the classes have gone and reveals that she is indeed pregnant, and will not be returning after the Christmas holiday.

'We'll be getting married, of course,' she says.

'It's not always "of course" these days,' I say.

'Oh, we mean to make it all fine and legal.'

'Why did you not tell us that you were engaged?'

'We decided to skip that and just marry.'

'In effect, you've rather skipped that too!'

'Maybe.'

'Was it Harris or Skye?'

'Harris.'

'Your Tir-nan-Og?'

'Oh, no, we've no inclination to make that our romantic home. It just suited us to meet there last summer. Ian is on a research vessel. But meanwhile, promise you won't say a word to anybody. I have a reason.'

'If you want it that way. Will I eventually be told the reason?'

'Oh, yes, as soon as our plans are mature.'

'You'll have to tell the Head – or maybe you've already done so?'

'No – not yet. Now it comes to the point, I'm going to hate doing it.'

'Why is that?'

'Don't know. Maybe I'm embarrassed. I've travelled up to school a number of times in his car. I suppose I could have told him then, but somehow I didn't. It's been since September – those days I was late – '

'Yes, of course, I remember.'

'I was wondering if – ' She looks at me questioningly.

'Yes?'

'Would you – I mean – do you think you could – tell him for me?'

'Tell him for you! Definitely not! I'm not all that much responsible for you. You must go along now, and tell him yourself. You needn't give the real reason. You could always say that you've suddenly decided to get married early next year and want to make preparations. But you should have given proper notice.'

'Oh, dear, I suppose I ought. But I thought he might make arrangements for a presentation. I'd hate that. They'd all have to know then.'

'I still can't see why they shouldn't.'

'Believe me, it's not *all* the Staff I'm thinking about. I'd like it kept dark for the present.'

'Oh, all right. You can always say that to Fergus Ogg. He's a man of the world – although he is a Headmaster.'

'Yes, I think he is. Look here – I'm sorry about all this. I've enjoyed being here. You'll have to get another teacher now.'

'You certainly won't be giving us much time to do that. But

I'm told they're coming off the assembly line a lot quicker these days, although it's maybe more for the Secondaries.'

'I'd like to go back and teach after I've been married for some years. They say teachers are to get scarcer and scarcer.'

'That would have been a lovely thought to have had when I qualified, but right now it's no comfort.'

Once we were so thick on the ground, we were always being tramped on!

Today Marjorie tells me that Fergus Ogg took it all very urbanely.

'Just what you said − ' she says. 'Oh, by the way, Shirley's off today. Bothered with her appendix, I think.'

Anybody off at this time makes inconvenience thrice inconvenient. I am glad to accord second encores to the strolling players to keep the classes amused while I struggle to remove the Christmas decorations from high up the walls in preparation for the holidays in two days' time.

This afternoon Fergus sends Ailie to take over Shirley's class, while Rory combines Ailie's and his own in a carol rehearsal for the Church service tomorrow. I explain to Ailie that Shirley had planned to fill a Christmas stocking for the class. Her idea was that this stocking was to be hung up empty before they departed today. Shirley has all the sweets ready in the cupboard. We open the baskets to take them out, but can find no stocking.

'Oh, just dole out the sweets and fruit as they are,' I say.

'Oh, no,' says Ailie. 'Hanging up a stocking is far better fun. I'll bring one this afternoon. Just you leave it to me. I've always rather liked teaching the Infants. I don't know why I ever stuck it so long in the upper classes.'

I am about to say that she might apply now for Marjorie's place, as I could do with an experienced teacher in Two B − but I remember my vow of silence in time.

In the afternoon Ailie says she has brought the stocking and she will get the children to hang it up with ceremony after we all return from Church and before the classes are dismissed.

For the first time perhaps in living memory there are no untoward incidents either going to, or coming from, the Church. This may be due to the fact that the Puddicks, the Gillogaleys and the Mullens are all off this afternoon, having 'bent' the holiday dates to suit their requirements. We know that their excuse tomorrow will be that they have just found out that the holidays didn't begin yesterday after all. And, of course, this will enable them to partake of the largesse from the Christmas tree – or the stocking.

Ailie rushes back into the empty classroom, when we finally have the school to ourselves, to fill the stocking before the Staff finally meets in the staffroom for their own Christmas cheer. She rushes out again some minutes later.

'Oh, dear!' she says. 'I never dreamt that would happen! But I didn't have an ordinary stocking.'

The oddest sight meets my gaze when I go into her classroom where earlier the empty stocking had been hung from a hook near the top of the blackboard. The stocking now begins two feet below the ceiling on the blackboard frame – but it continues down the whole length of the board a full ten feet to within an inch or two of the floor. It is an extraordinary sight, for it looks as full of bumps throughout its length as a boa constrictor that has just swallowed a succession of rabbits.

'Good Heavens!' I say. 'What's that?'

'I've never filled one of my stockings before,' says Ailie, her voice full of surprised awe. 'You see, I've got varicose veins and all my stockings are made of elastic!'

We have our Staff Christmas party again this year, and this time it is enhanced by a Christmas tree from Rita's classroom. Around the tree are piled a number of parcels, for we have all shopped for gifts for one another, including Fergus and Rory.

Rita's classroom cooker has been retained and repaired and is now working, so we have heated mince pies. Fergus and Rory bring the intoxicating contraband and a box of chocolate liqueurs as well. 'French –' says Daphne in a knowing whisper.

When the parcels are opened, Fergus and Rory have acquired no fewer than five and four ties respectively, while the female staff exclaim with delight at pairs of nylon stockings for each.

'That'll reveal your occupational disease,' says Vera.

'What's that?' says Daphne.

'Varicose veins,' says Vera.

'It's me that's got the veins,' says Ailie. 'But I can always wear the nylons on top of my elastic stockings.'

'That will look really glamorous,' says Vera. 'What shade are yours, Daphne?'

'Gun metal,' says Daphne.

'Appropriate,' says Vera.

'What shade are yours, Vera?' asks Daphne.

'Forever amber,' says Vera.

'Never heard of it. Is it a brown?'

'No, it's a wicked – '

We are interrupted by the proposal of a toast by Fergus, 'To the Cinderella of all professions!'

'That reminds me,' says Ailie, fishing among the perennial pile of jotters on the windowsill. 'When the *Cinderella* show was on last week I gave my class a composition to write about it. Read what Jeanie Burke has written.'

The jotter goes the rounds. And what Jeanie has to say is this:

'Cinderella just hated every minuet of her life.'

January
1952

It is our first day back after the Christmas holidays.

I am met at the foot of the glaciated steps by Charlie Chapman and Augustus Ponsonby.

'There's been burglars!' says Charlie, the relish of excitement in his voice. 'They breaked in when the school was shut!'

'There's a policeman taking notes,' says Augustus. I think this description is applicable to Augustus himself.

'The polis is my uncle,' says Charlie proudly. 'He's a sergeant.'

'Ah!' I say. 'I see the law is on your side, then, eh?'

'It's on me Mum's side,' says Charlie. 'Me Mum's brother.' They escort me up the steps and they are full of reporter's zeal to enter the building before the bell rings. But Barney is there, and shoos them off.

'The bell will be late,' he says. 'They've left an awful mess. You never saw the like!'

A river of ice issues from our staffroom into the corridor. I am also cut off from my classrooms by it, temporarily, I hope, but certainly until this minor glacier has been melted by the slow heat that Barney has been hours setting in motion.

'They turned on the tap in the lavatory, and your whole staffroom's a mass of ice. I arrived up yesterday to get the furnace going and found the whole place frozen up. Maybe it was a mercy that it was frosty, otherwise there'd have been a terrible flood.'

'It's turning to a flood now,' I say, skipping over the runnels. 'Where's the Staff?'

'Along in Mr Ogg's room. He says you're all to use his room until this is cleaned up.'

When I reach the Head's room most of the Staff are already there. We wish one another a Happy New Year!

'How did they get into the school?' asks Ailie.

'By a fanlight in the corridor near my door,' says Rita.

'Only children could get in by that fanlight,' says Rory. 'We'll soon find them.'

'St Bride's brats again,' says Daphne.

'More likely an inside job,' says Rena.

In less than an hour the Sergeant has traced the burglars. Involved are a Gillogaley (no show without Punch), a Puddick, and four boys from Homeston Primary just over the Burgh border in Greeninch. Borderline cases all.

Missing is every scrap of blackboard chalk, several feathers tweaked from my pheasant's tail (plus one wing slightly detached), a bag of scones which Daphne forgot to take home before the holidays, two pairs of ancient chalk-encrusted shoes from the box of teachers' working shoes in the cupboard, and a tin of money belonging to Vera.

The tin contained Vera's collection of money for teaching counting. Vera always believes in the real thing. There was, she assures us, a lot of farthings, ha'pennies, pennies, threepenny-bits and sixpences in the tin. It is not the loss of the money she mourns, however, but the tin. She says it was a Royal Jubilee tin from 1935 which she had received as a child. A kind of antique, you know.

An antique, forsooth! I gave out tins like that in my classroom in Garlock St at that same Jubilee!

Bambi Puddick, she goes on to say, knew the whereabouts of this tin, and that the cupboard had a defective lock.

'But haven't they all?' says Rita.

The usual scribbles, cartoons and signatures on the blackboards reveal the culprits even to us, by which token the big Sergeant does not appear as astute as he did at first. After all, what would BP stand for, if not for Bambi Puddick? It takes no more than five minutes for BP to be turned inside out and the names of his confederates disclosed.

The most heinous act of the Heatherbrae chimpanzees is the turning-on of taps. Daphne with sadistic wit says this warrants the laying-on of hands. It keeps us out of the staffroom for two days until the ice-cap has receded.

Daphne's voice is raised in complaint when finally we are re-installed and she has found her forgotten bag of milk scones missing from the staffroom cupboard.

'I was so late the day before the holidays, I just couldn't go back for them.'

'Oh, forget it,' says Rena. 'What good would they be to you now anyway? The burglars must have broken a few teeth on them.'

'Hard as bricks they'd be,' agrees Rita. 'Serves them right.'

'Last year,' says Vera. 'It was Westminster Abbey that was burgled. The Scottish Nationalists stole – or rather – removed, the Stone of Scone.'

'That's right,' says Rita.

'And this year,' says Vera solemnly, 'Heatherbrae has lost its scone of stone.'

Rita throws one of the jotters from the windowsill at Vera. They alone are untouched by the flood or the burglars.

We are again out of our staffroom today, as there has now been discovered the seasonal burst pipe in the lavatory, and we are threatened with the Second Ice Age, although the first is hardly dry in its tracks.

'I suppose,' says Daphne, 'we'll have to share the Head's room again with the men.'

'With your married experience,' says Rita, 'that should give you no problem.'

'I find it very embarrassing,' says Daphne.

'Embarrassing?' says Rita.

'Oh – well – you know. It's that key that hangs behind the door.' In Fergus Ogg's private room there is no lavatory as in ours. A key which hangs on a hook near his back door gives access to another door in the corridor outside next to the room-and-kitchen, and within is a WC and wash-basin.

'I hate having to take it down off the hook in front of them,' says Daphne.

'If that's all you ever take down in front of them, you've no need to be so modest,' says Vera.

'You're really very coarse,' says Daphne distastefully. 'What I'd like to know, is why Marjorie's left.'

'Has that anything to do with your last remark, or are you just changing the subject?' says Vera.

'Yes,' says Ailie, 'why has Marjorie left? Very sudden, wasn't it? I hardly realized she'd left with all the upsets we've had these last few days.'

'Well, why did she leave?' says Rita, looking at me.

'Who told you she'd left?' I ask, stalling.

'The Head told me,' says Ailie, 'when he asked me to take over her Infant class permanently.'

'I'm delighted at that,' I say diplomatically. 'I did mention you might possibly be willing to do it when you took over a class prior to the Christmas holidays.'

'What about Marjorie?' persists Daphne.

'I believe,' I say, 'that she became engaged during the holidays. She was leaving to get ready for her wedding. It's to be quite soon.'

'Did you ever?' says Daphne. 'Of all the close clams, she's one. Seems to me a very hasty decision. Suspicious, in fact.'

'Oh, everything's suspicious to you,' says Vera bluntly. 'Everybody doesn't go around showing off their rings. First your suspicion rests on Fergus, now it's on Marjorie.'

'And,' says Daphne, fending off this barrage, 'I shouldn't be surprised if the two are connected in some way. Remember what I heard in Skye last year. And wasn't Marjorie in Skye that same summer?'

'A lot of imagination,' says Shirley, who comes in just then to take up the cue. 'Fergus Ogg is far too old for Marjorie.'

'He's younger than I am,' says Daphne, naively.

'And that definitely makes him too old,' says Shirley irritably as she goes off to her class.

Fergus meanwhile is taking Ailie's Primary Six class himself. Not from pure zeal only. He is trying out some Intelligence Tests, and this gives him a chance to work it out as he wants to. At least, that is what he says to me today when he presents me with a formidable folder of Tests designed for infants.

'That's the Stanford-Binet,' he says, as if they were incunabula. 'I'd like all the entrants tested at February's enrolment.'

'Will we be using the results for anything special?' I ask, knowing that St Swithin's are now doing this to control the demand for admission to the Eton of Greeninch.

'Eventually it will help to elucidate some other information I'm gathering. Actually, I only want certain selected children's statistics. But to save conjecture, I propose doing them all. It saves unwarranted suspicion as well.'

'M'm – yes,' I say, doubtfully.

'I should like the list of problem families, and here are reports to be made out for them, and for anybody else you think is capable of learning but doesn't.'

And he leaves me my homework for the next few weeks piled up on my desk.

It may be the menace of Intelligence Tests or the change of

environment, but Ailie all this week would have been more aptly called Wailie. Her voice is raised plaintively in both classroom and staffroom.

'I'm afraid I'll be no good at all this Intelligence Testing,' she says. 'We never had them or these IQs either when I began. I can't see how it's going to make them any better at their lessons.'

'It won't make them any better,' I say.

'Then why –?'

'It will show the level of each pupil compared to the average.'

'But I know the level of each pupil already,' she says.

'Most of us do,' I concede. 'But this may reveal intelligence where you have not suspected it. Sometimes, for many reasons, intelligence is hidden.'

'It's hidden mostly,' she says. 'And I can't see how these tests will bring it out.'

'They have been proved very reliable,' I say, having to range myself on the side of the management, 'but you won't be asked to carry them out. I'm doing them for the whole Infant Department.'

'I see. I'm not likely to do it right?' she says sniffily.

'Fergus Ogg asked me to do it.'

'Did he? But it's all so unnecessary, like so many of these modern things.'

'Times are changing,' I say, which is the biggest cliché of all time.

I am thinking it would be a catastrophe if she decided to change too – into a retired teacher. Until someone else is appointed I must endeavour to retain her. Better, I think (to comfort myself), than having Daphne in the Department. I wilt at the very thought.

'Of course,' says Ailie, either as the result of thought-transference or with blackmail in mind, 'if these new-fangled things become too much, I can always retire.'

I mention my hopes of another teacher to Fergus Ogg, who says he has applied for one already. There seem to be no unemployed teachers these days, desperately driving trains, or tramcars, or slaving in mines as there were when I was newly-qualified.

January is a bad time of the year, apparently, for any newly-hatched teacher. Like butterflies and wasps, they don't come out in any strength until the month of June, and then the Secondaries are netting them if they are graduates. And even if they are not, induced hatchings of semi-skilled pupae, officially called 'emergency-trained', are still taking place all over the country, to meet the post-war boom in babies.

Neither Fergus nor I look with any kindliness on that emotive word 'emergency'. I try to visualize what an emergency teacher would look like, but fail.

Emergencies, however, take different forms, like witches. The weather has softened itself down again, and the perma-frost at Heatherbrae has melted and made everything spongy and wet. Sore throats, coughs, colds, influenza and sheer depressed spirits at creeping to school on winter mornings has decimated the classes. Excuse notes in the usual variety of forms, sizes and colours arrive on my desk as if I were the editor of *The News of the World*.

Bobby Farquharson heads the queue presenting petitions this morning. He comes on behalf of his brother Reggie who was enrolled last August. Mrs Farquharson, who lives in a semi-detached villa behind the school and whose husband is a chief draughtsman in one of the local ship-yards, writes:

'I am sorry Reggie won't be back today after all. He threw off the germ he caught last week in a few days, but my husband caught it on the rebound and he has held it so long that he has been off the yard for four days. I really thought Reggie had parried it successfully, but it seems he has been hit all over again.'

Cricket or football?

I thank blear-eyed Bobby who goes off to his class. But I hear that he is absent in the afternoon. Stumped, I suppose. And so it goes on all week.

I am hoping that one of these 'emergencies' is not lying-in-wait till the imminent enrolment, as I shall need every member of Staff present to hold down the veterans while I enlist the raw recruits.

I have hastily looked through the 'Stanford-Binet' and think that if every individual child is to play through all the rows of little pictures, shapes and oral questions, it will take weeks to test both them and the other classes. I go along to ask Fergus if we could begin before the actual admission day and get as many 'done' as possible.

'We could try out, say, half a dozen,' he says. 'It will let you get it down to a fine art before the big show begins.'

'Do we ask the parents to bring them along?'

'Ah – that's a snag. If we do, it might get around and cause panic in Heatherbrae. They'll think we're a new St Swithin's.'

'We'd better wait until they are enrolled then.'

'Maybe. But you can take your time, and work through them at your leisure . . .'

Leisure?

Ailie is again prophesying doom in the staffroom, now dried out. New linoleum in a draught-board pattern has been reluctantly laid since the melting ice brought out the very worst in the wooden floor below, in the form of a mouldy odour impossible to live with. Daphne had prophesied a rat there, but this ambition of hers was reduced to some spots of dry rot with which she had to be content. The paleolithic linoleum had also been so destroyed by the melting glacier that even the Repairs Department could invent no means of deflating the big blisters that rose all over it. Rita thinks that the draught-board pattern is appropriate, since she sits between the door and the window. Ailie thinks it makes the room look tasteless, a strange pronouncement, as what it never had it would surely never miss. It is nicknamed from the start 'Your Move', as we're seldom on it long enough to contemplate the design.

Ailie has a new fear today. Since joining the Infant Staff she has had several, the last being almost a neurosis, brought about by the vast quantity of lost bits from the constructional toys, knobs, screws, bolts, pins, sticks, ball bearings and wires. These are somehow always missing at the end of the day, and this is not alleviated by numerous pieces being found just at the last minute and brought to her after all the boxes have been stowed away. The first week this nearly drove her crazy. That week I nearly lost Ailie along with the bolts and screws. She almost decided to flit back again to Primary Six, which from this distance seems a simple and more desirable organization, of screwed-down desks in neat rows and jotters in neat piles, than the colossal work-shop of the Infant Department. From which it can be seen that the Primary classes above Primary Two are still primitives.

Today I am partly relieved to hear that she is on another tack.

'I think,' she announces, 'that it must be nearly time for our Triennial.' She says this in the same tone of voice as 'Time for your Quinine!'

'What on earth's a Triennial?' says Shirley.

Ailie looks at her as she would a nestling tapping its way out of the shell.

'To me,' puts in Vera, 'it always sounds like some sort of herbaceous plant.'

Ailie turns to Shirley. 'Inspectors usually visit schools every three years to make a thorough inspection.'

'Oh!' Shirley sounds alarmed. 'Thorough? They don't miss anything, I suppose you mean?'

'Seldom,' says Ailie, with relish.

'Oh, dear,' says Shirley, 'I'd better let my appendix know – '

'How horrible!' says Ailie, recoiling. 'But you won't know the day nor the hour, so you can do nothing about it.'

'Oh, shucks!' says Vera rudely. 'You make it sound like death. Anyway, the Inspectors are better-mannered these days and give the schools notice. And if the Head's just as well-mannered, he tells his Staff.'

'Is that so?' says Ailie. 'Changed days.'

'Yes, isn't it?' says Vera, 'and high time too.'

'If it's anything like the last time they came,' says Rita, 'it will be a sheer anti-climax. They just chatted away about – '

'Toilet rolls,' I cannot resist saying.

Ailie looks shocked.

'What I think,' says Rena, 'is that Inspectors are on the way out. Anachronisms – that's what they are.'

'If Daphne was here she'd be asking what that was,' says Vera.

'I suppose if you're one yourself, you don't notice who else is,' says Rena.

'You're all a catty lot,' I say. 'But I agree that Inspectors all seem to have had a tranquillizing drug lately. They're very mild and benevolent all of a sudden. Advisory bodies.'

'And that's the first sign of decadence,' says Rena. 'They're fast becoming an effete race, and will be more or less extinct by 1975. As soon as they become nice, their day is over.'

'I've a feeling,' says Rita, 'that Headmasters are not what they were either.'

'I won't hear you say a word about the Head,' says Ailie. 'A pleasanter gentleman you couldn't meet. He was always so good at taking over my class. Nobody ever does that now.' I sit, tacitly reproved.

'Oh, I agree entirely,' says Rena, 'but he's more and more of an official, and less and less of a teacher. If it weren't that we were so short of Staff just now, he'd not be out of his room.'

'You mean his office,' says Vera. 'That's what the Head's room is called in some schools. The Head's just becoming an extension of the Administration.'

'Mark my words,' says Rita. 'It'll not be long before a secretary walks in carrying a typewriter. There are schools that have them already.'

'In fact,' says Shirley, 'it seems to me that if it goes on like this, teachers will be anachronisms themselves. That will be interesting to see.'

'I hope I'll never see it,' says Ailie.

'You can always retire,' says Shirley.

I don't think Shirley should put that idea into Ailie's head. She might do it, then Shirley would have two classes.

'You're too fit to retire,' I say flatteringly.

'I didn't feel like that yesterday,' says Ailie. 'Trying to get these Infants to learn their tables.'

'Tables!' I can't help bursting out with this. 'You don't need to teach tables to Infants. Few have the least clue about multiplication. All that went out with the Ark.'

Ailie looks so shocked that I feel sure her resignation will be in tomorrow.

'I ought to have told you,' I say apologetically. 'They don't begin them till Primary Three – or even Four. It's a bit different now.'

At this point Daphne comes in. 'Did I hear you say something about tables? Is this the next thing to be axed?'

'No axing,' I say patiently. 'We work with things – materials, you know. It's for Fergus to say what's to be done further up the school.'

Shirley is still looking apprehensive. 'Tell me,' she says to Ailie, 'about this Triennial affair. 'Is it really to happen soon?'

'It either makes you or mars you,' says Daphne.

'Don't listen to that,' says Rita. 'This is 1952, not 1932. You'll see we'll have fewer and fewer Triennials, if any at all. You'll see it will be mostly Intelligence Testing.'

As a stone thrown into the staffroom pond, this makes its circles.

'My class,' says Daphne, 'doesn't need any Intelligence Testing.'

'The Headmaster thinks otherwise,' I say. 'But don't get alarmed. It's only for his own research, I understand. Nobody can change the intelligence of pupils. It's a constant.'

'I don't agree,' says Daphne. 'Some of mine were much better when they left my class last session than they were when they came into it.'

'That's got nothing to do with innate ability,' says Rita.

'The Headmaster thought my results were good,' says Daphne. 'He took them away to study.'

Rita looks exasperated. 'Among the piles of forms on his desk, they are as nothing,' she says. 'Headmasters are doomed.'

'What about Infant Mistresses?' I ask, curious.

'They are doomed, too,' says Rita, 'to become spoon-feeders, nose-wipers and baby-minders.'

On the Heatherbrae bus today there is another conductress. She looks long and hard at me when she comes round with the tickets. I hold out my fare, but her gaze is fixed on me.

'D'ye no' mind o' me, miss?' she says at last.

'I know your face –' I say rather vaguely, 'but . . .'

'Och!' she says, 'surely ye mind o' Tillie McTavish!'

'Tillie!' I say. 'Of course!'

Well do I remember Tillie McTavish, although she spent almost as much time in the toilets of Garlock St School as she did in my classroom there.

'How long have you been on the buses, Tillie?'

'This is me first day – me first job.'

'Surely not your first since you left school?'

'Well, ye see, I got married –'

'To anybody I know?'

'Aye – tae Obadiah McCaig. Ye mind o' him?'

'Who wouldn't? And how's Obie getting on?'

'He's gettin' back soon, to labouring in the yards. But it's gettin' dearer to live, so I thought I'd take a wee job mysel'. I've got a wee lassie –'

'Really?'

I begin to feel like a centenarian.

'We're in a council house up in the Heatherbrae Scheme, so she'll be el – illegible for your school.'

'I'll be very pleased to enrol her. The enrolment day is at the beginning of next month.'

'I'll bring her up to ye, then,' she says.

I proffer my bus fare, but Tillie waves it aside with a grand gesture.

'No' frae you, miss,' she says and goes back down the gangway to take Bridie's policeman's fare.

Ailie is still with me in the Infant Department, although precariously. Fergus Ogg has insisted that she remains here until after the February enrolment. I am relieved at this, as it turns out to be a large enrolment, over thirty, more houses having been built on the slopes behind the school, and the post-war Bulge becoming a barrage balloon.

Among the entrants is Wigmore R Gardiner, second son of the yellow-gloved Walter P Gardiner, who has confidently introduced him to me as extremely intelligent, and one who has been doing Intelligence Tests since the age of three. He is a bespectacled boy in an out-moded navy-blue serge suit. Wigmore immediately finds his mental level in Claudius, the latest Romanesque member of the Ponsonby family.

In marked contrast to the erudite Gardiner and Ponsonby families, comes the child of Tillie McTavish, or rather, Mrs Obie McCaig. She is a dusky-haired little lass in a neat blue jumper and skirt.

'Here's wee Daphne,' says Tillie. 'She's to have free meals just for today and tomorrow. We filled in a form for free meals when Obie was unemployed, but now he's in work again, so she'll no' be having them free after tomorrow.'

'Where will she be having her meals after that, since you're working?'

'She's to go to Obie's mother.'

'I thought she lived away up at Hillwood.'

'She did, but she was lonely up there wi' the family away in Canada.'

'In Canada?'

'Aye, they all emigrated except Obie. They're gettin' on fine too.' The years, the years. Although I do not yet say 'Eheu', since the present crowds in too much.

'Why didn't you call the wee one Tillie?'

'Oh, Tillie's such a common name, miss. But Daphne – that's real romantic. There's just something I have to mention as it were, miss.'

'Yes, Tillie, what's that?'

'She'll maybe have to get oot noo and then to the toilet. I'd be obliged if ye'd let her, miss.' Hereditary characteristics?

February
1952

I have begun the Intelligence Testing, since the beginners' class is not in session in the afternoons just now. But it is an uneasy peace, as I feel that Ailie is less and less enamoured of the way we do things nowadays. Yesterday Shirley was absent, suffering from what she calls a grumbling appendix. Because she had to take on an extra half-class, Ailie has done more grumbling than the appendix, and no operation of mine seems to cure it.

'The sooner you get a younger teacher the better,' she says. 'If it wasn't for that nice man Fergus Ogg asking me to stay on, I'd retire tomorrow.'

Rory today has Primaries Six and Seven in one vast mob, as Fergus is away again at a meeting in the Administration Offices. He is there along with all the other office boys, with a view to thrashing out the vexed question of the Eleven Plus. This leaves his school to struggle with the Eleven Minus this afternoon.

'A little thrashing in the school instead of at the Admin Office might be more useful,' says the bloodthirsty Daphne.

'The parents are complaining about those that don't pass the Test,' says Ailie.

'Of course!' says Rita. 'They wouldn't complain if they did pass.'

'The whole sin of the teachers,' says Rena, 'is that they still think it's good to be intelligent.'

'I can see the day fast approaching,' goes on Rita, 'when it will be a sin to encourage the clever ones in case it offends the failures.'

'Nature thought of that,' says Vera, 'so she didn't make too many clever ones, otherwise they'd be assassinated through sheer jealousy.'

'There may be something in what you say,' says Ailie, 'but in my day nobody dreamt of complaining. Those that were top were top and those that were bottom were bottom, and that was that.'

'It's like the Grand Old Duke of York,' says Vera. 'But that's all too simple. I think we should concentrate on the half-way ups. They're the ones worth salvaging and improving.'

'Quite right,' says Rita. 'Those at the top can generally look out for themselves, and those at the bottom will defy your efforts.'

'We'll let Fergus work it out,' I say. 'He's the man for the research, if he can find time for such a hobby these days.'

Today Fergus has indeed found time for other things. It is revealed to us dramatically. This morning Daphne flounces into the staffroom, her whole attitude one of aggression. She slams her handbag down on the table and almost makes a hole in her hat as she hangs in on her peg.

'Well!' she says. 'That finishes it!'

But it is not the hat she means.

'I'm to go down and take one of your Infant classes,' she says, as outraged as if she were going down to teach in Barney's furnace-room.

'I did not ask for that,' I say.

'And you may be sure no more did I,' she says. She whirls round upon Ailie. 'You're to blame,' she goes on, 'asking for a transfer of class in the middle of the session.'

'This is the change-over of classes,' says Ailie. 'This is the right time to transfer.'

With all his harassments on his head, it seems that Fergus has omitted to inform me of this catastrophic transfer of tyrants. But the massing of resources for what promises to be a prolonged campaign is as suddenly suspended.

News is brought today, by Daphne herself, as always a dabbler in doom, that the Provost's wife has just died. This apparently is of such momentous importance to Daphne that yesterday's problem shrinks in significance.

Both Fergus and Daphne are away this afternoon at the funeral. The school timetable is also altered to bring the children into school earlier, and before the coaches begin to line up beside the Provost's lamp-post across the street.

Rita thinks that Daphne's interest extends considerably beyond her past friendship for the Provost's wife.

'Can you imagine,' she says, 'Daphne in the part of a Provost's wife?'

'It is very unbecoming,' says Ailie, 'to discuss such matters today. Daphne was very rude to me yesterday, but even so, I don't think we should make such conjectures.'

'I'll bet,' continues Rita undeterred, 'that Daphne has herself made these conjectures. In fact, I expect she's already planning what she'll wear at the Coronation.'

'Coronation!' says Ailie in a shocked tone. 'The King's not long dead himself.'

'I'm sure,' says Vera, 'in view of your argument yesterday, that nobody, not even you, Ailie, would object to Daphne being crowned!'

'I don't see,' says Ailie naively, 'how Daphne could ever – '

'As a Provost's wife,' explains Rita patiently, 'she could be going to London next year for the great event. I expect the Provosts will all be invited.'

'I don't know how you think up all these ideas,' says Ailie.

'Some of the Scottish Nationalists are up in arms about Elizabeth being called the Second,' says Rita.

'The Provost across the street isn't a Nationalist,' says Ailie. 'He was very much against all that blowing up of pillar-boxes.'

'Anyway,' says Vera flippantly, 'it would be nice for Daphne to see the Scone of Stone in its original place.'

'I really think you should wait till the Provost's wife is buried before you make any more outrageous suggestions,' says Ailie.

'Still,' says Vera, ignoring this advice, 'I'll bet that as soon as Daphne gets home tonight, she'll take her ermine stole out of its moth-balls.'

Daphne is definitely sweeter this morning, having, she tells us, partaken of three sherries and much funeral baked-meats after the obsequies.

'We all went back to the Provost's house,' she says, 'although Fergus said he simply couldn't, for he had so much to do in the school. As I was a very close friend of the Provost's, Fergus winked an eye at my having the rest of the afternoon off.'

We all wink an eye at that. I think we should also wink the eye if she were to be off tomorrow too, as she is due to come down in the world to Primary Two B. Shirley is back, and so Daphne can be closeted with Two B all to herself.

Before the classes assemble this morning, Fergus Ogg seeks me out.

'I'm sorry I didn't give you notice about Mrs Whyte's transfer,' he says. 'I know she doesn't like it, but it may not be for very long. I'm hoping to get another teacher.'

'Oh, that would be fine,' I say.

'Mrs Whyte told me this morning that there's a lady come to live next door to the Provost. Apparently she's a teacher, and would like a post in one of the schools. She's from England, but was brought up in Australia, I think. I'll try and find out more. It might be better than nothing. Only temporary, of course.'

Later, Daphne says to me, 'I expect you heard that I may be able to find another teacher for you.' Her voice has the ring of a DOE about it.

'Fergus did mention it.'

'I put in a word to the Provost about it there and then, as soon as I heard a teacher had taken the house next door. She's supposed to be a qualified teacher too. Of course, knowing how short we've been lately, I immediately snapped her up. So you have me to thank for that.'

'We'll have to see her first, and what her qualifications are.'

'Oh,' says Daphne, 'she'd do well enough for Infants.' This really gets my birse up. But I exert superhuman control.

'She ought to have the special Diploma. In fact, anybody who teaches Infants ought to have it.' The birse takes over just then. 'And that goes for you too,' I say.

'Well! Do you hear that?' she says. 'Here's me doing you a good turn, and that's all the thanks I get.'

'We'll defer the thanks,' I say. 'I strongly suspect your Provost's next-door neighbour will be one of those Emergency-trained types that are being churned out just now.'

'This is an emergency, isn't it?' says Daphne.

March

After some unproductive investigations by Fergus, he reluctantly introduces the new teacher to me.

'Penelope Bissell,' he says. 'Mrs Bissell understands she is here strictly on a temporary basis. And,' he adds, forebodingly, I think, 'her appointment can be terminated at any time.'

Another Mrs on the Staff. This will surely dilute Daphne's importance as the only married woman. But she can hardly object, as it is obvious that it is because of Daphne's own disinclination to teach the Infants that Mrs Bissell is here at all.

Ailie is now installed again in Primary Six and Daphne in

Primary Five, and the status quo is restored, except, of course, with me.

It is the status of Penelope Bissell herself that puzzles me. I look at her and see what we call here in Scotland, a woman like a 'skelf', very small and thin, something like a pipe-cleaner, and wearing very tight clothes. Her only concession to the northern winter (still reluctant to depart in March) being a huge top-heavy fur hat that looks as if it came straight out of Alaska.

'Bill, my husband, brought this hat back from Canada on his last voyage,' she says.

'Your husband is alive, then?' I say.

'Oh, yes – just. He almost wasn't.'

'Why was that?'

'He was washed overboard last time at sea – but he was saved.'

'What kind of – ?'

'He's in trawlers.'

'I see. Dangerous job.'

'Yes, isn't it? – We're going to be divorced.'

(What, Daphne, are your widowhoods compared to this?)

'About your qualifications –' I begin.

'I taught in England for a year – after I came back from Australia. It was a crash course.'

'Crash course?'

'That's right. Took six months, it did. Same as the baby.'

'Have you a baby?'

'It miscarried.'

'Sorry.'

'Oh – don't be. With all this mess about Bill and me, it was a mercy.'

'You live alone, then, in the house across the road?'

'Oh, dear, no. Patricia and Priscilla are there too. They're running a guest-house.'

(Guest-house? Next door to the Provost?)

'Guest-house?'

'What's wrong with that?'

'Nothing – only, have you any guests?'

'Two sales representatives, one car salesman, – oh, and a

bookie. Nice boys. Say, that's a nice boy you have for a Head teacher. Real smasher. Is he married?'

'Only to his job, so far.'

'That's maybe because there's nobody in his school that sets him alight.'

I am temporarily quelled.

'What system did you use,' I say, striving to come back to basics, 'when you taught reading?'

'Oh, you don't teach reading to the five-to-seven-year-old age groups.'

'Really – don't you?'

'Oh, no. Maybe later, if they want to.'

'What do you teach them, then?'

'How to live,' she says.

'I'm sorry to have to sweep aside your theories,' I say, bringing up the howitzers, 'but you'll have to teach reading here. And counting. And writing. And after they've managed to survive your efforts, they'll have learned how to live. This is a school we have here – not an out-back.'

'I was never a teacher in the out-back. Only after I came to England.'

'From what you've just told me, England sounds like an out-back to me.'

'When do we get paid?' she asks.

I take comfort in the thought that Fergus Ogg underlined the word 'temporary'. In that special Course I took some years ago in Infant Methods, there wasn't a single word about what to do about Penelope Bissells.

I am chary about leaving Penelope Bissell alone with Primary Two B. It is with great trepidation that I shut the door upon her and leave her to do her worst.

I hear strange noises emanating from the classroom throughout the morning, but adhere to my determination to let nothing interrupt my own work which has suffered so much for days.

At the interval I ask, 'How did you get on with the reading?'

'Grand! Say, can't they read!'

'Did you hear them all?'

'A boy called Walter heard all the boys, and a girl called Fiona heard all the girls.'

(I wonder to myself what a girl called Penelope did.)

'And who,' I ask, 'heard Walter and Fiona?'

'They heard each other.'

'What other lessons did you do?' I ask, fascinated.

'They like hearing about the kangaroos.'

'Ah! A nature lesson?'

'Is that what you call it? We always called it Biology.'

In the staffroom Penelope is regarded as being more in the nature of a kangaroo herself. She is a jumpy, squirming eel of a girl, never settling in a chair, always perching on the table and laughing like a kookaburra. The only time she is quiet is when she is drinking a bottle of school milk through a straw.

'I'm going dancing tonight,' she announces, jumping off the table and executing a few steps with a wiggle of the hips.

'Where do you dance,' asks Vera; 'apart from the staffroom, I mean?'

'At the Palais.'

'You don't mean *The Silver Comet* surely?' says Ailie, horrified.

The Silver Comet, once an unsuccessful picture house, has lately been gaining notoriety as a dance hall, the clientèle being known, to those who live up at Heatherbrae, as the riff-raff.

'That's the place,' says Penelope. 'I think I'll be going with Digby tonight.'

This morning there is a question curling like smoke in the air of the staffroom.

'It could have been a mistake, of course,' Daphne is saying, 'I really thought she was all right. But Humphrey is having second thoughts too, since he heard about the boarding-house.'

Humphrey?

Before she can say any more, Penelope prances in and puts her big fur hat on Daphne's peg.

'I'm going to the Coronation next year,' she announces. 'It'll be a real thrill. Any of you going?'

'It's a big expense, going all that way to London,' says Ailie.

'That's what Digby says – but I'm saving up to buy a new outfit. Now that I'm teaching, I can do it. I'm going to buy a new car for Digby as well.'

The bell rings just then, leaving the questions unanswered.

Shirley whispers to me as our Infants are coming in, 'Who is Digby?'

To which I reply, 'And who is Humphrey?'

All is very quiet this afternoon, and I am continuing with the Intelligence Testing. I have just finished with my fifth victim when I hear an almighty thump. It seems to have come from Primary Two B's classroom. I make towards it hastily.

When I open the door, Mrs Bissell is lying prone on the floor beside her high chair which is out in the middle of the room with children sitting all round it.

I rush forward and wonder whether it will be smelling salts or splints. I have scarcely decided which, when up jumps Penelope.

'What on earth – ?' I say weakly.

'Poetry lesson,' she says, grinning.

'Poetry?'

'Just showing them how Humpty Dumpty fell off the wall.'

Crash course!

Criticism of Daphne has been displaced by criticism of Penelope. Everybody is wondering how much longer I can stand her. I decide to find out how much longer she anticipates being paid for showing them how to live.

'By the way,' I say this afternoon, 'I'll be taking some of your class away for an Intelligence Test.'

'I've made a study of Intelligence Tests,' she says. 'I could do it for you.'

'Did you really? When was that?'

'On the course.'

'Special studies take years.'

'Oh, that was a preliminary only. When I go up to the University I'll be taking up Psychology in depth.'

'When will that be?' I ask eagerly.

'Oh – well – first of all I've got to get three Highers. English, Maths, and maybe French.'

'Do you mean to say you haven't got any of these?'

'No. I'm studying for them. Digby keeps me back a bit – but I should manage after another year.'

'And then – ?'

'Oh, then I'll be going to Oxford – '

'Oxford?'

'Yes, or somewhere, to get my Degree.'

'That will take another three – maybe four – years.'

'That's right. Then I'll be taking a Degree in Education after the B.A.'

'That makes another two years, maybe three –'

'Then a special Psychology Course?'

'And then your Teacher's Training Course– the real one.'

'I'm looking forward to it.'

'By the way, how old are you?'

'Twenty-seven last year.'

'Nearly twenty-eight, shall we say. And you've another eight years before you get all these lovely qualifications. That will make you thirty-six, won't it, when you're finished? Almost a pensioner.'

'Oh! I never thought about it like that. Will I really be thirty-six then?'

'Unless you can get suicide courses in them all, you will.'

'I must talk about it to Digby tonight.'

'By the way,' I say, 'who's Digby?'

'One of our lodgers,' she says. 'A smasher!'

April
1952

Humphrey, we discover after the Easter holidays, is the Provost.

And the boarding-house, according to Daphne, has been empty for a fortnight. The Provost – Humphrey – thinks there has been a moonlight flitting of the three Disgraces, as Daphne now calls them. Penelope fails to turn up today.

'You won't, I'm sure,' says Vera, 'see hoof or horn of that one again.She had an impermanent look about her.'

Ailie pronounces her epitaph: 'She was a very vulgar girl with no Certificates.'

Daphne is silent on the subject, but voluble about her anticipation of delights to come.

'I'm hoping,' she says, 'that I can get away for the Coronation next year.'

Rita looks at me and winks. 'I suppose,' she says to Daphne, 'you'll be getting your robes ready.'

Daphne laughs as near to delightedly as she ever comes.

'Oh – well – I'll not be the one wearing the robes. But Humphrey now, I expect – '

She tails off so that we can fill in the details for ourselves.

'The ermine is really only rabbit,' says Vera.

'Humphrey's ermine is real,' says Daphne. 'It's got all the wee black dots on it.'

'Fancy that!' says Vera.

'Even the peers and peeresses don't need to have real ermine any more,' says Rena. 'It's quite *au fait* to have rabbit instead.'

'*Au fait* – ' Daphne opens her mouth, but shuts it again quickly.

'The ermine is to be simulated ermine,' goes on Rena.

'I must tell Humphrey,' says Daphne.

'If we're still short of teachers, I can't see anybody getting off for the Coronation,' says Ailie.

'But we'll surely get the day off,' says Daphne.

'Of course,' says Ailie, 'but you can't go to London, see the Coronation and get back all in the one day – at least not comfortably.'

'You bring stools and sit on them all night eating sandwiches,' says Vera.

'I feel neither Humphrey nor I will be sitting on stools,' says Daphne.

'I may as well say now,' says Ailie, 'that I have every intention myself of going to the Coronation, nevertheless.'

'Pluggin' the school, Ailie?' says Vera.

'Oh, no. I'm going to retire.'

'Really?' we all say.

'Yes,' says Ailie, 'in June this year. I don't think I could stand any more of these Intelligence Tests – and these group methods – and Speech Therapists – and all these Gym things – oh, and lots of other ideas that are supposed to be the coming things.'

'What other things?' asks Daphne.

Do I detect a quaver of alarm?

'Oh,' says Ailie, 'residential schools! I'd hate to be sent to a residential school. Imagine sleeping with the Gillogaleys?'

'They're usually for deliquents,' says Vera. 'Much worse than the Gillogaleys, although I can see your aversion to having even them overnight.'

'Is that what they're for?' says Ailie. 'What a lot of money it must cost, feeding the worst like that.'

'By the way, Daphne,' says Shirley. 'Where are you thinking of going for your holidays this year. Skye again?'

'Not sure yet,' says Daphne. 'Skye's not ruled out, but it depends on how – things, you know – turn out. I could be thinking of – well, other islands besides Skye.'

'Such as?' says Vera.

'Oh – Capri, perhaps.'

'Tiberius lived there,' says Vera innocently.

'So far, I don't know anybody who lives there,' says Daphne serenely. 'But one must broaden oneself, I suppose. There's another place I fancy too – still farther afield.'

'Where's that?' asks Vera.

'The Canaries,' says Daphne. 'Of course, if I go, I shall fly.'

Today I am presented with another assistant. She is in marked contrast to Penelope, for she is about sixty years of age and wears an unfashionable tweed skirt and a bulky jumper. Fergus introduces her as Mrs Mann. She has had fifteen years' experience of teaching, all in the days before she was married, and she has not taught since. She will 'fill in' for us, Fergus says, until June.

I conduct the motherly Mrs Mann to Primary Two B and give her a sketchy outline of the morning's work. I warn her against using any of the building material – or painting – until I have time to show her how to manipulate it and thus avoid tears (her own). She is very apologetic.

'I know it's bound to be different from the days when I taught,' she says. 'But I'll do my best.'

I notice that Mrs Mann has a very pronounced 'Kelvinside' accent, which in the West of Scotland means snobby-polite. On the other hand, she somehow inspires confidence, and is, after Penelope, an oasis of serenity.

I feel, however, that for the last six weeks I have been conducting a Training College for Teachers rather than an Infant School. The only thing we have not so far had sent for our sins is a student. I forbid myself to contemplate it. Then I mentally retract. I think of myself as a student and how the teachers virtually gathered their garments around them and shrank away from us in disgust.

It is the season for students, too, as the summer vacation is imminent and they are being sent out to all the schools like free samples. But oh – please – not one just now!

I am delighted with Mrs Mann. She has been with us now for a fortnight and is already the most popular teacher in the school, not only with Two B, but also with Rory's 'Project' class which she has to take on Tuesdays and Thursdays. Francis Gillogaley, Sam Mullen and Marigold Puddick are her adoring slaves.

The Bulb Show, foreshadowed in the autumn by Fergus, is upon us, and Mrs Mann has thrown herself into preparations whole-heartedly. So many entries have been received that the Town Council, who are sponsoring it, have had to use the Town Hall to stage it. The Provost has been very active in encouraging it.

This puts Daphne in a peculiar position, a dilemma, in fact. The Provost – Humphrey until now – has accordingly asked her to give her services at the Town Hall on Saturday afternoon. Daphne's class has planted no bulbs and has no exhibits. No use, she had said, planting bulbs in a school. They go mouldy near the hot pipes.

We ask, 'What hot pipes?'

Daphne, with the grimmest expression of martyrdom we have yet seen, prepares to sacrifice her Saturday afternoon while we all go off on our usual end-of-week relaxations.

Today, Friday, therefore, rows of little boys and girls carry bulb bowls out to the playground. Fergus and Rory are to transport the bowls in their car boots to the Town Hall, but there are so many that Fergus says we should have hired a van.

The teachers have been asked to appoint porters for the loading and unloading. Ailie calls them 'monitors'. Mrs Mann calls them 'managers'. Ailie appoints her star pupils, George Mc-

Cartney and Martin Edwards. Mrs Mann, who has Rory's Project class today while Rory is on this other business, appoints Francis Gillogaley and Sam Mullen.

'They'll smash every bulb we have,' says Daphne.

'I thought your class didn't have any,' says Mrs Mann.

'I'm talking generally,' says Daphne.

'I'm sure,' says Mrs Mann enthusiastically, 'Frencis and Ser. will be mervellous!'

Ailie has still half a dozen bowls to be transported after a number of journeys have been made. She is trying feverishly to stake up the top-heavy hyacinths with knitting-pins.

'Oh, don't use knitting-pins,' says Mrs Mann. 'Frencis and Sem whittled big twigs for ours.' And she produces workman-like natural stakes and ties them up expertly with garden twine. They look very handsome as they are stowed in the boot of Rory's car till four o'clock when he promises he will make the last delivery at the Town Hall.

But before four o'clock Elijah Puddick has fallen off the wall which divides the boys' playground from the girls', and has broken his leg, he thinks. Rory's car is off to the hospital with a chastened Elijah inside.

Comes Monday morning, and it is a day of spates, of prize tickets for hyacinths, daffodils and tulips, waved under my nose before I can reach the school door. Spates of congratulations from me.

Spates today also of tadpoles. It has been a beautiful sunny week-end, ideal for hatching tadpoles. There are six jelly jars on the desk. Wigmore says, 'The tadpoles will die.'

'Not at all,' I say.

'They will,' he persists, 'unless they have pond-weed in the jars. It says that in my encyclopedia.'

Wigmore, of course, could read before he came to school, which did not, contrary to his father's belief, make it easier for me. I am thinking of promoting him and Claudius up by two moves into Two B.

It is an interrupted day. A large basin has to be found to accommodate the tadpoles. Wigmore says that he himself will seek out the pond weed. The bowls are also being brought back from the Bulb Show, and these are set out for collection in Rory's room. A constant stream of bearers moves along the corridors all morning. The traffic problem is not facilitated by Bobby Burke finding a newt in the playground at the interval and bringing it to me in the classroom in his hand, all the time attended by a dozen supporters. We put it in one of the vacated jelly jars.

'There are two baby sparrows at the room-and-kitchen,' says Bunty Puddick. 'Bambi is bringing them round.'

It seems we have founded a zoo.

Wigmore regards the sparrows with an expert eye. 'They fell out of a nest above the annexe,' he says. 'A pair of birds have a nest under the roof.'

With the help of Francis Gillogaley and Sam Mullen, suggested as the steeplejacks by Mrs Mann, and a ladder kindly lent by Barney, who gives physical support to the ascent, the fledglings are duly returned to the nest.

Summer terms are changing their nature. Attempts at lessons are somehow abandoned in favour of seasonal excitement. Mrs Mann is a natural-born exponent of the modern expediency, but she is successful.

Ailie is complaining that her six bowls of lovely bulbs, so expertly staked by Mrs Mann, have not been returned from the Town Hall.

'Who brought back the others today?' I ask.

'Fergus Ogg had a van deliver the lot this morning,' says Rita. 'They may still be down at the Hall.'

'Oh, no,' says Ailie. 'Mr Ogg phoned down and they weren't there. He phoned the other schools too, and they all said they had brought back only their own.'

'And I'm sure they must have won prizes too,' Ailie says. 'They were exceptional.'

And it turns out that they would have won prizes had it not been that when Rory went to put his sports equipment into the boot of his car for the boys' football match, the six bowls of bulbs were still there, and in no condition to win any prizes by that time.

'Blame Elijah Puddick,' he says in mitigation. 'I clean forgot the bulbs.'

'I'm thankful,' says Ailie, 'that I'm going to retire. Nobody does anything right any more.'

Mrs Mann has different views.

'That Primary Seven of Mr McTavish's,' she says, 'are cute little creatures.'

'Try your patience to the limit, they would,' says Ailie. 'Delinquents, that's what they are. Very difficult to control too.'

'Oh, no!' says Mrs Mann. 'Speak politely to them and they'll speak politely to you. Take Sem now – Sem Mullen, you know. I just say to Sem: "Sem, me boy, you just say 'thenk you, Mrs Menn' when I give you your jotter," and Sem says "thenk you, Mrs Menn" as polite as you like.'

'What about the Puddicks?'

'Oh, you mean Merigold? I like Merigold – and that dear wee Bembi as well.'

'Little devil,' says Daphne.

'Quite a cherub,' says Mrs Mann. 'He amuses me.' And nothing can alter her opinion.

'Do you get far with teaching them?' asks Rita, 'they're pretty slow.'

'Oh, yes, the Project idea appeals to them, and to me too.'

'What Project are you doing?' ask Rita.

'Hem and eggs – and fish and chips.'

'What!'

'Mr McTavish left it to me to choose something homely and work it out from there. What could be more homely than your breakfast?'

'Well, I'm blowed!' says Vera.

'We're going up to Heatherbrae Ferm next week,' continues Mrs Mann, 'to see the pigs that produce the hem, and the hens that lay the eggs, as well as how the potatoes are grown for the chips. We're going fishing some day too.'

'You'll be cooking them next,' says Rita.

'I'm hoping to do that,' says Mrs Mann. 'Haven't you a cooker? Do you think we could use it one day?'

May

I receive a letter this morning, from Marjorie. It is written from an address in Glasgow. In it she tells me she has a baby boy, and that she and her husband, Ian, are thinking of emigrating to Canada. Ian has heard of a likely post in the Ministry of Agriculture and Fisheries. But the second part of the letter is perhaps the more interesting:

'I said to you,' she writes, 'that I should eventually tell you why I left the school in all that rather melodramatic secrecy. Summed up – my husband, Ian, is one of Mrs Whyte's step-children! I am sure that will surprise you.

'Ian and his sister Caroline are children of Mrs Whyte's second husband, and they were nearly grown up when Mrs Whyte entrapped their father (Ian's words). They both left home as soon as they were through College. Both of them vowed never to go back or have any communication with Daphne after that. Caroline is a teacher and is now married and living in Germany, sufficiently far away from the wicked stepmother. Ian and I met at an inter-College dance about four years ago. Just now we are living in Glasgow with my mother's sister, because Ian's Headquarters are here.

'I shall be going soon to visit my mother in Greeninch, but I shall certainly not visit Heatherbrae, for the best of reasons. In spite of that, I thought it was a great wee school and I enjoyed being there from the teaching point of view. I shall be sorry not to see you all again, with one exception.

'If we go to Canada, I shall certainly write to you. Maybe word of our activities will eventually reach you at Heatherbrae. I expect there must have been some trenchant remarks passed when I left so precipitately. Fergus Ogg was just marvellous – and you too. I mean to write to him as well some day soon.'

210

'Marjorie,' says Rita today, 'has had a baby!'

For once shock has stunned Daphne into a long silence. You can see quick calculations going on behind all the eyes looking at Rita as she makes this pronouncement.

'She was such a nice girl too,' says Ailie.

'She's still a nice girl,' says Rita.

'She did get married,' says Vera.

'I knew there was something underhand going on,' Daphne says at last, coming out of her state of shock. 'I knew that girl would come to no good.'

'She has come to quite a lot of good,' says Rita. 'A good husband and a lovely baby.'

'It's Marjorie's business,' says Shirley, 'and anyway, what difference does it make?'

'She was one who would take any man at all,' goes on Daphne. 'Anyway, who is the man? That's what I'd like to know. And I might be able to make a fair guess as to who the father is, and it's not necessarily the one she's married.'

'Really!' says Vera. 'Did you ever hear such a made-up story! Has nobody any facts?' She turns to Rita. 'Who told you, Rita?'

'Marjorie herself,' says Rita. 'I met her in Greeninch at the week-end. And you can forget Daphne's fantasies. Marjorie and her husband and child are probably going to Canada.'

'Just as well to clear out under the circumstances,' says the implacable Daphne.

'They're not clearing-out, as you put it,' says Rita. 'Her husband is very likely going to a job with the Ministry of Agriculture and Fisheries. I think she said her husband was a research scientist.'

Daphne's mouth has fallen open, but no more sound issues from it.

'Yes,' says Rena, 'she did mention, I think, that they were in Harris last year because his ship was there at the time.'

'Would that be where – ?' begins Ailie, and stops. Then she goes on, 'I don't know what schools are coming to these days, what with First Assistants neglecting their duties and children walking all over the school all day, and now probationers – you know . . .'

'Supplying the future material for you to teach – sorry, for us to teach. You're retiring. Anyway, Marjorie was no longer a probationer when she left. She'd done her two years. Let's send a card to Marjorie!'

'Good idea!' says Rita. 'She had the forethought to give me her address in Glasgow, although a letter would have reached her by her mother.'

'I'll do it,' I say, 'if you let me have the address.' I decide at present to say nothing about my letter.

Later, I ask Rita if Marjorie mentioned what her married name was.

'Oh, yes,' she says, looking hard at me, and giving a Vera-like wink. 'It's Whyte – spelt with a "y". What do you think of that now?'

The Town Council, having got their Bulb Show off their chests, fling themselves whole-heartedly into the Council Elections. All this week we have had 'pamphlet litter' under the desks, collected avidly over the week by the children and finally discarded over Barney's playground. Barney, who seldom utters disapproval, is so wrathful that he almost emulates old Gurney.

The teachers have a grouse too. Our little school was not used for the Elections, so we did not get a holiday that day. The Gillogaleys, the Puddicks and the Mullens take a holiday in any case, although only for half a day. The Attendance Officer was on their track and had them back in the afternoon. Marigold asserts she was 'canvassing for the candidate'. Whereupon Rory gives her a composition to write on 'Ward 3 on Polling Day', just in case Marigold's canvassing was done in Woolworth's.

The repercussions of the Elections are beginning to be felt. To-day three workmen arrive from the Burgh Works Department and proceed to remove the Provost's lamp-post. 'Humphrey', alas for Daphne, is 'out' at this Election. His term of office has expired and he seeks no re-election.

The whole school attends the uprooting of the lamp-post. A van stands by to receive it when eventually the giant is reverently exhumed.

'Where are they taking it?' This question I hear being asked as I penetrate the crowd to recover my Infants, who now come back in the afternoons. They are well-embedded in the crowd. Barney is meanwhile vigorously ringing his bell and Rory blowing his whistle like a referee.

A voice nearby says, 'It's going up to Hillwood.'

'But that's a Council Scheme!' I hear a Rosetree Avenue accent protest.

'That's right,' says the first voice. 'This year's Provost isny a snoot in a villa. It'll be grand seeing it in front o' a cooncil hoose for a change.'

Daphne and Ailie are both outraged at the ignominious disappearance of the symbol of bourgeois power from across the street.

'It looks so empty,' says Ailie.

For Daphne, whose disapproval for once is less voluble, all her dreams of velvet, ermine and gold chains of office together with honeymoons on Capri or the Canaries are fled in company with the Burgh lamp-post.

This sad silence is shattered by the announcement of a Staff meeting. Staff meetings are not an addiction with Fergus Ogg. Some Heads have a Staff meeting complex. Power neurosis, Vera calls it.

Fergus Ogg has hitherto been considered normal – until today.

'Is it about the Prize-giving?' asks Ailie. 'I found it a bit of a strain last year.'

'Maybe it's a concert.'

'The Lord forbid. It's too near the end of the term for that, surely.'

'A show of work?'

Groans.

'I think,' says Mrs Mann, who is a spy in Rory's camp, 'that it is a Sports Day.'

'I wish I'd retired at Easter,' says Ailie.

'I can see us,' says Rita, 'getting all the names for all the races, collecting money, running the heats, practising for the events. Awful!'

'And it's to be in the McTaratan Park,' says Mrs Mann, who is the only enthusiast, bar Fergus and Rory, 'kindly offered by Sir Alastair, I believe.'

'All that equipment to be carried there,' bleats Ailie.

'Oh no,' says Mrs Mann, 'Mr Ogg is hiring a van, and we're all to go in buses.'

Murmurs of mollification.

'Don't ask me to supervise a marquee,' says Daphne, shelving her responsibility before it's hatched. 'I hate struggling with urns.'

'Funerary?' says Vera.

'If that's a new kind, I'm still not having anything to do with it,' says Daphne, to Vera's great delight.

'Oh, no tea!' says Mrs Mann. 'I've offered to supervise the eats, which are to be ice-cream and lemonade and potato crisps.'

'Good!' says Rita. 'I now look upon it with a less jaundiced eye.'

'All very well for you,' I say, 'but the Infants are the worst at a Sports Day. Our Sports Day will begin tomorrow and go on until the day dawns. And you never know what will happen on the field of battle.

We practise every day with skipping ropes. Little girls can use skipping ropes but little boys trying to use them comprise a comedy act. So the boys concentrate their energies on eggs and spoons. Besides these, there will be a flat race for all.

The Egg and Spoon race takes intensive coaching. Shirley and I have the greatest difficulty explaining that the egg should not be steadied on the spoon with a finger. At first the boys run blithely forward, and immediately all the eggs fall off. Wigmore reveals that he has an Achilles heel when it comes to sports, especially the

Egg and Spoon race. His egg falls off all the time and he stands and looks down at it as if he had just laid it himself.

Claudius wins the practise race every time, until we discover he has fixed a tiny piece of plasticine by sleight-of-hand to the spoon.

'Big cheat!' shouts Daphne McCaig, and then immediately falls on her nose as she takes off recklessly for the skipping-rope race.

Claudius laughs. Daphne weeps. Wigmore is defeated. And nobody wants a Sports Day.

June

The river is ethereal blue, and in the Park high above it the sun drenches the grass and makes it so green that it is calling out to be run, jumped and fallen upon. This the children do as soon as we reach it. For today is no practice event, but the real Olympics.

The teachers are like hens with broods of crowded chicks chirping round their legs.

'Where,' says Shirley, 'are the toilets?'

'Glad you mentioned it,' I say. 'I see Daphne McCaig wildly waving a hand. But we're to line up the Infants immediately. No time to go up to the toilets till the first race is over.'

Mrs Mann comes up. 'The toilets,' she says, waving a hand towards them, 'are at the other end over there – just beyond the finishing tape.'

We begin lining up the girls for their flat race. All toes are to the line marked on the grass.

'Now,' I say, 'watch Mr McTavish. As soon as he drops his flag, run! Everybody ready?'

Daphne McCaig waves an urgent hand. 'Please – '

I hasten over to her. 'Look,' I say. 'The toilets are just over there beyond the tape, where Mrs Whyte and Miss Steele are standing. You'll be finishing there, so just go right on. Got that?'

Daphne nods her head, and shifts from one foot to the other. I can see Mrs Whyte and Rita Steele, one at either end of the tape. They will grab the first three winners and get their names.

'Now!' I say.

Rory drops the flag. It is a breathless moment. The small girls, always a popular turn, are urged on by the cheers of the rest of the Primary.

'Go it, Bunty.'

'Lick them flat, Daphne. Hey! Look at wee Daphne – '

In no time at all, the race is won. Wee Daphne breaks the tape yards ahead of the others. Her objective is the toilet. She hares right in, regardless of Daphne Whyte, who fails to grab her in her urgent flight. I see Daphne Whyte chasing Daphne McCaig into the Ladies' Toilet. Incentive is all.

'At least we'll be finished first,' says Shirley behind me as we line up the boys with the eggs and spoons.

'Keep your hands off the eggs!' shouts Shirley. The flag drops. The china eggs drop too, onto the grass as if from prolific hens. They are pecked up by the scoop method by small boys with anxious eyes and furrows on their foreheads. Reggie Farquharson seems to be leading. Close behind him comes Wigmore. Good learner Wigmore, I think.

Then there is a sudden pile up of boys, eggs and spoons on the home stretch. It is such a bad pile-up that Rita and Daphne desert the tape to loosen the victims from the scrum. They dart back again as Wigmore (first) and Reggie (second) romp home the winners. A long way behind comes Claudius.

Wigmore is dancing on the grass in glee.

'Look!' says Shirley, as finally the Infants' events are over. 'There's a photographer from the *Greeninch Graphic*. I see Daphne Whyte moving in his direction. See! She's talking now to Fergus. You'll be seeing her in the papers tomorrow. Pity it won't be in colour. Did you ever see such a magenta dress?'

'Jealous?' I say.

The Infants go to the tent for ice-cream and lemonade. Daphne McCaig has paid three more visits to the Ladies' before we reach the end of the repast. Excitement at being a winner?

'What a waste!' says Shirley, 'pouring lemonade into Daphne.'

Claudius comes up to me.

'I was second,' he says, 'in the Egg and Spoon race.'

'Not at all,' I say, 'it was Reggie.'

'It wasn't,' says Claudius, 'Reggie was first.'

'It was Wigmore who was first,' I say.

'Reggie was first, I was second, and Bobby Burke should have been third.'

'Oh, nonsense. You go and ask Miss Steele. She took your names.'

'She didn't see,' persists Claudius, 'that Wigmore was holding on his egg with his finger.'

'We've no proof of that,' I say.

'Miss Steele didn't see, because she went to help the boys who fell.'

Complaints like this are numerous on Sports Days. It will have to be sorted out when we get back to school.

'I'll look into it,' I promise Claudius. The aggrieved tuck into their ice-cream. Wigmore looks belligerent.

At the end of the day, when the noise of battle and triumph of victory have departed the field, we are back in the staffroom. If there were any couches to flop on, we should all flop.

'The thought of a show of work on top of that makes me think of retiring, too, Ailie,' says Daphne.

'You've a few days to recover before the show of work,' says Rita.

'My sewing will take more than a few days,' says Daphne. 'Such lazy girls I have this year. I'll have to take home most of their work and finish the trimmings myself at the week-end.'

'What have they made?' asks Mrs Mann, who is the only enthusiast about Shows and Sports.

'Knickers,' says Daphne. 'Twenty-six pairs. I hope I'm not asked to do them next year.' She looks significantly at me.

Everybody is craning her neck this morning to see everybody else's newspapers. The photographer from the *Graphic* has done a comprehensive job, as has the one from the *Bulletin*, the Glasgow-based newspaper. The rather inferior newsprint of the *Graphic* does little, however, for either complexions or sartorial efforts.

Daphne comes in bearing a copy of the *Graphic*. She hurriedly opens it. Her face is wreathed in seraphic smiles.

'Look,' she says. 'Isn't that good? I just happened to be talking to Fergus at the time.'

'Is that you?' says Rena. 'I thought it was Ailie.'

'It's my dress,' says Daphne. And she takes scissors and cuts out the photograph. 'I wonder if Fergus has seen it.' As for me, I wonder if Fergus will also cut it out of the paper – hastily.

Vera gives a shout. 'Have you seen the one in the *Bulletin*? There's one of you in it too, Daphne.'

'Is there? And the *Bulletin* has a much wider circulation than the *Graphic*,' says Daphne. 'May I have a look?'

'Talk about candid cameras,' says Vera mischievously. We all go forward to look. Daphne is rigid.

'A scandal! That's what it is,' she shouts. She turns to me.

'That was all your fault. That awful child should have been made to go to the toilet before the race began.'

'There was no time,' I say weakly.

'Think!' says Mrs Mann. 'That wee girl would never have won but for her pressing need. It was a famous victory.'

'I'm going to contact the *Bulletin* and complain. I'll have that removed.'

'*Fait accompli*, Daphne,' says Vera. Daphne stumps out of the room. The picture she is going to complain about shows Primary One Girls reaching the tape, but in the background it also shows Daphne Whyte running into the Ladies'. There is no sign of Daphne McCaig who was being chased and beat her to it.

'There's another interesting picture farther on,' says Shirley, 'which I should say provided evidence for a court of appeal on behalf of Claudius Ponsonby.'

She points to a shot of the finish of the Egg and Spoon race, and Wigmore romping home, with an unmistakable finger holding on his egg.

I take the newspaper to the classroom.

Daphne is disappearing out of the school gate as I come down the steps at four o'clock this afternoon. She is carrying a suitcase.

'Going for the week-end?' I ask as we proceed down the road.

'Week-end! This case contains my girls' sewing for me to finish up for this awful show of work.'

'I hope it rains, then,' I say.

'I'll have to get my sister to help me,' she says. (Daphne generally does.) 'I'm staying with her in Greeninch till Monday.' And she makes towards the railway station.

'I'm having to go on the train,' she says. 'It's awkward travelling on a bus with a big case like this.'

The show of work is to be on Tuesday evening. This afternoon, Monday, we clear the rooms and put up backgrounds on walls and desks for the articles to be shown.

Daphne comes into the staffroom and dumps down her suitcase.

'Took me all week-end to get all these finished,' she says. 'Jean and I had to put the elastic in more than half of them.'

'Let's hope it doesn't let them down,' says Vera.

At the interval Daphne is distracted.

'I don't know what on earth to do,' she says.

'What! Has the elastic burst already?' says Vera.

'No – oh, no. I'll have to go round to Mr Ogg and see if he'll let me away at once.'

'Away?'

Rita explains.

'Daphne took the wrong suitcase from the rack in the train this morning. It wasn't till she went to lay out the sewing that she found all the knickers were away to Glasgow.'

'Oh, dear!' says Ailie. 'Whatever will you do without your knickers?'

'It's as well it's summertime,' says Vera. 'And what was in the case you took in place of yours?'

'Dozens and dozens of men's trunks and – eh – those Athletic Support things. I suppose that's what you call them.'

'It was just a slight change of sex, as you might say,' says Vera. 'Daphne had hung up one or two pairs before she realized that they were not what they were.'

'There must surely have been a commercial traveller in the same compartment,' I say.

'I was in a terrible hurry,' says Daphne. 'The men in the compartment were all reading newspapers, so nobody seemed to notice. That case was exactly like mine.'

Daphne is so upset that finally it is Mrs Mann who seeks out Fergus and explains the crisis.

'Mr Ogg has phoned Glasgow Central Station,' she says when she comes back. 'I expect that whoever went off with your – eh – knickers will have found his mistake by this time. Oh, that sounds awful – but you know what I mean.'

For the rest of the day, the Whyte crisis is grist to Vera's mill, but, by the end of the day, the suitcase is reported as being held at Glasgow Central Station, where the lady who took the men's underpants may call for her property.

Married experience has never been mentioned once, and complete with suitcase, Daphne catches the 4.15 pm train for Glasgow.

The show of work has come and gone and prostrated more than Daphne. We are all thankful that the arrangements for the Prize-giving will devolve mainly upon Rory McTavish and his minions in Primary Seven.

Meanwhile I have the job of arranging for Ailie's presentation, and also for the refreshments that are to follow the Prize-giving. The first passes off with many sighs from Ailie, who is wildly anxious to retire on Sports Days and shows of work, but is full of emotional nostalgia and regrets, when it comes to making her final speech of renunciation. She takes her tea trolley from the Staff, her china tea-pot from her dear Primary Six as well as a hideous tea-cosy from Daphne, a personal present from the one who is now the most experienced member of Staff, she says.

'When do you go off to the Canaries – or is it Capri?' Rita is asking Daphne this morning at the interval.

'Oh, I'm not going there – this year. Going back to the Hebrides – Isle of Mull this time.'

'Maybe Fergus has an establishment there as well,' says Vera. 'Did you ever get to the bottom of that mystery?'

'He took care to choose a remote place,' says Daphne, 'where nobody could ever be sure of what was going on.' Mrs Mann comes in during this speech.

'Am I missing some gossip?' she says.

'It's about our Headmaster,' says Vera. 'According to Daphne he keeps an establishment on a remote island.'

'How thrilling!' says Mrs Mann. 'Who lives in it?'

'Daphne thinks his children.'

'More and more interesting. By the way, did anybody ever hear any more about those Intelligence Tests he was doing?'

Rita and Rena come in and light up cigarettes.

'Still discussing Fergus's peccadilloes, eh?' says Rita. She and Rena look at one another and laugh.

'Going on another snooping holiday, Daphne?' says Rita. 'You unearthed some goings-on last year.'

'By the look of you two,' says Vera, 'something is going on.'

'True enough,' says Rita. 'Your mystery is solved. I have Bambi Puddick in my class this term and today he was bursting with news. This year all the Puddicks are going away for a holiday. For your information, Daphne, it seems they'll be "breaking the silence of the seas among the farthest Hebrides". Bambi tells me they are all going to Skye. And what's more, the Gillogaleys and the Mullens are going too!'

'I', says Daphne, 'am going to Mull – thank goodness.'

'How can they possibly afford it?' says Ailie. 'They're feckless people.'

'They're all going for free!' says Rita.

'Free? What lunatic is taking in a lot of hoodlums like them?' says Daphne.

'Fergus Ogg,' says Rita.

We all look at one another.

'Bambi says they're all going to live in a great big house away up in the sky,' says Rena.

'We asked Fergus about it,' says Rita. 'He confesses he's been running an experimental school for slow learners and deprived families. First it was only in the summer holidays as a try-out. But now he is thinking of extending it and employing regular staff.'

'He must have lots of money,' says Ailie.

'I feel sure,' says Rita, 'that Fergus has never been entirely dependent on his salary. He dropped a hint that he had inherited the "establishment" from his rich uncle – and enough to run it. He said it laughingly, but I suspect it's true.'

'I'd never have had the nerve to ask him all those questions,' says Ailie.

'So far,' goes on Rena, 'it's only one school, not two "establishments" as the rumour said. Although he did say he was thinking of trying to get a house eventually on the mainland.'

'I should have thought,' says Shirley, 'that an island would be safer to keep the Gillogaleys on.'

'Devil's island,' says Vera.

'He's still working on research connected with running residential schools like these,' says Rita. 'I think the Intelligence Tests had some bearing on it too.'

'And,' says Rena, 'the Education Committee are apparently blessing the venture. The new DOE is going himself to see it this summer. But Fergus doesn't want the blessings of officialdom just at present.'

'What have you got to say to all that, Daphne?' says Vera. 'It destroys the plot of your nice Gothic novel, eh?'

'If he thinks he'll reform the Gillogaleys or the Puddicks or the Mullens, he's mistaken. Bad they are and bad they'll always be, residential fal-de-rals or not.'

'They're not really such bed kids,' says Mrs Mann. 'I think it'll be ebsolutely mervellous for them all going to Skye. I wouldn't mind lending a hend myself.'

When I go back to my classroom, Daphne McCaig and Bunty Puddick are standing at my desk.

'Can I go to the bethrowm?' says Daphne.

'The what?' I say.

'The bethrowm,' says Daphne.

'You mean the bathroom?'

Daphne looks at Bunty as if waiting for instructions.

'We say bethrowm now,' says Bunty. 'It's more polite.'

'Who says so?'

'Merigold's teacher makes the class speak polite now. We were playing at a wee school last night and Merigold was the teacher. She was acting Mrs Menn.'

'I hope,' I say, 'that she grows up as nice as Mrs Mann, whether she speaks like her or not.'

Daphne runs out to her bethrowm. Bunty lingers.

'Is there something else you want to say, Bunty?'

'It's about the tadpoles.'

'Yes?' Bunty had previously offered to take one of the jars home for the holidays.

'I'll no' be takin' the tadpoles noo,' she says, all fine talk gone to the winds. 'We're goin' away for oor ain holidays – for two months.'

'That will be fine,' I say. 'We'll find someone else to take the frogs, if there are any left by then. Where are you off to?' I add innocently.

'Heaven,' says Bunty, 'so we canna take ony tadpoles.'

The final act of the term, the Prize-giving, is almost an exact reproduction of last year, except that, instead of a Boy Scout, there is a handsome naval lieutenant in uniform, the son of Sir Alastair McTaratan. The Lieutenant is big and breezy, and shakes hands with his right. This time Cecilia McTaratan is to present the prizes. Along with these advantages, I have another, consisting of an extra six inches of space from the edge of the platform. I am thus able to relax and enjoy the event. Daphne McCaig's mother has decided to keep Daphne at home today – in case she disgraces you, miss.

'We're going away at the Fair to Dunoon,' Tillie says, 'so Daphne'll no' break her heart when she's no' at the Prize-giving. She'd never get a prize for anything, anyway – except maybe for running.'

Fergus rises to thank the Lieutenant for his speech, which has gone down a treat with everybody, especially Primary Seven, where every boy is going to join the Navy, and every girl marry a lieutenant. The cheers are tumultuous.

To the surprise we have all felt at Fergus's research programme is added another. After the Prize-giving is over, two bottles of champagne have appeared on the table in the refreshment room, along with the repast supplied by Fergus, even more sumptuous than the one we had last year.

'Champagne, forsooth,' says Vera. 'Inherited his uncle's wine cellar too, eh?'

Glasses are duly charged. It is then that Fergus asks us all to drink a toast – 'to Cecilia, my future wife!'

As I go down the flight of steps that help Heatherbrae dwellers to reach the main bus route, I meet Mrs Puddick and Mrs Mullen on the way up. Mrs Puddick is wearing a pair of blue carpet slippers and carries two heavy shopping-bags. Mrs Mullen has again 'done something to herself', for her hair now falls to her shoulders in a bouncing long bob. She carries a patent leather handbag. Mrs Puddick stops and puffs as I am passing them.

'Hope you have a nice holiday, miss,' says Mrs Mullen.

'I'm sure your children will be looking forward to Skye,' I say.

'Wee Elijah's no' goin',' says Mrs Puddick.

'What's happened to him now?'

'He swallowed a sixpence last night.'

Expressing hopes that Elijah's sixpence will turn up in time for going to Skye, I go off down the steps.

Aboard the bus, who should be the conductress on duty but Tillie McCaig!

'Not off to Dunoon yet?' I say.

'Tomorrow,' she says. 'You on holiday noo?'

'That's right,' I say, holding out a sixpence for my fare.

With queenly disdain, Tillie ignores it and goes down the gangway to bell the next stop.